All Scripture references taken from the KJV of the Holy Bible, unless otherwise indicated.

<u>THE SCARCITY MINDSET:</u> ***When Nothing Is Ever Enough – Even When It Is***

by Dr. Marlene Miles

Freshwater Press 2026

Freshwaterpress9@gmail.com

ISBN: 978-1-971933-56-6

I0835101

Paperback Version

Table of Contents

THE SCARCITY MINDSET

When Nothing Is Ever Enough – Even When It Is

INTRODUCTION: The Handbag

Some years ago, I sent my sister three designer handbags. Three. If I had different relationships with the others, perhaps I would have sent one to her and one to each of them, but I didn't. I sent all three to her. She received them, thanked me, and that was that.

About six weeks later, she contacted me to tell me that one of the designer handbags had broken, and she wanted to exchange it.

Exchange it? Six weeks later, after using it already? I told her it was past the exchange date, and I asked her, how do you break a designer handbag? I have never heard of that. It wasn't the highest-end bag—it was Coach—but those are not shabbily made.

She said it was the strap.

So, I told her to take it to a cobbler and have it repaired. And in my mind, I thought, Use one of the other two. They were free. Use the bag you were using before you got the three free ones.

Why are you complaining?

We didn't talk much about it after that.

But the question stayed: *Is anyone ever satisfied?*

WHERE IT COMES FROM

Scarcity did not begin with you. Before it showed up in your habits, your reactions, your conversations, and your quiet calculations, it lived somewhere else first. It lived in environments where there was not enough. Not enough food. Not enough money. Not enough certainty about tomorrow. It showed up generations before you learned how to stretch, how to ration, how to make something last longer than it was ever designed to last. Your own ancestors may have learned how to watch closely, measure carefully, and avoid waste at all costs. Those were not bad instincts. In their time, those instincts were necessary.

The Great Depression forced families to survive on very little. Jobs disappeared. Banks failed. Food was not guaranteed. People who lived through it learned to save everything—string, jars, scraps—because everything had potential value.

Go further back and you will find the Great Famine, where entire populations faced starvation. Scarcity was not a mindset then. It was reality. If you did not manage what you had carefully, you might not make it.

So yes—some of what you see today has roots. It was learned. It was modeled. It was passed down.

Here is where things shift. What begins as survival can become habit. What begins as wisdom can become rigidity. What begins as necessity can become identity, which is much harder to question.

A child watches a parent conserve, stretch, and calculate. That child does not always inherit the *reason* for the behavior. They inherit the *behavior itself.* Over time, the environment changes, but the behavior remains. The pressure is gone, but the posture stays.

Now the same patterns show up in places where they are no longer required. A person counts what should simply be enjoyed. Measures what should be received. Questions what should be appreciated.

And often, they cannot see it.

This is the Scarcity Mindset. It is not always loud. It is not always obvious. But it is consistent. It shows up in how people handle money. How they receive gifts. How they respond to abundance of anything, money, food, even attention. How they behave in small, everyday moments that reveal something much deeper.

This book is not about people who have nothing; it is about people for whom nothing is ever quite *enough.*

WHEN *ENOUGH* WAS LOST

In the beginning, there was no lack. In the Book of Genesis, man was placed in a garden where provision was already established. Food was not a question. Survival was not a concern. There was no calculation, no stretching, no rationing. Everything that was needed was present.

There was no scarcity. There was enough. More than enough. There was abundance and no lack. Man did not wake up wondering how he would eat. He did not measure portions or guard resources. He did not negotiate for more or fear receiving less. Provision was not earned. It was given.

Then something changed.

Through disobedience, access was lost.

The ground was no longer effortless. It resisted. It required labor. It produced thorns and weeds. What had once been freely available now required sweat and toil.

From that moment forward, man was introduced to a new reality:

Work to get. Struggle to maintain. Uncertainty about tomorrow. This was not just a change in environment. It was a change in experience. Over time, that experience shaped thinking.

When provision is no longer guaranteed, people begin to measure, guard, calculate, anticipate loss, or maybe even imagine and prepare for the worst. They learn to hold tightly because they have known what it feels like to not have enough.

Here's the problem with that: What was introduced as a condition of the world eventually became a condition of the mind. Even when there is enough… the mind does not always register it. Even when provision is present… the posture of lack remains.

This is the Scarcity Mindset.

Man has a tendency to forget, but he doesn't forget things that affect his sense of survival. This scarcity mindset is not simply the result of having little, it is the result of being shaped by loss.

Once that shaping takes place, it does not automatically disappear when circumstances improve.

A person can move into abundance… and still think like they are in lack. They can receive freely… and still feel deprived. They can have more than enough… and still behave as if something is missing.

Tension begins where the environment says, "there is enough," but the mind says "there is not. A person's behavior will follow the mind, not the reality. Your mind is uprising and trying to take over – to 'save your life' and your life isn't even under threat.

That is how scarcity continues. It is not because provision is absent, but because perception has not been restored.

This book is about that gap. The gap between what is available, and what is believed. The gap between provision and the inability to experience it as enough.

The unprospered soul will not remember how God, or that God… that soul will remember the threat, the uncertainty, the fear and how they, themselves did everything, with the help of their powerful mind to save their own life.

The devil doesn't have to mess with you physically. If he can reprogram your mind, your memory, your expectations, he can get you to ruin things for yourself, yourself.

THE *spirit* OF NOT ENOUGH

There's a particular kind of hunger that has nothing to do with survival and everything to do with perception. It doesn't show up as empty cupboards or missed meals; it shows up as a quiet, persistent sense that something is lacking—even when, objectively, nothing is. It's the feeling of not having enough: not enough money, not enough security, not enough time, not enough recognition, not enough life. Unlike physical hunger, this one doesn't resolve when it's fed; it often grows.

What makes this state so disorienting is that it isn't confined to scarcity. It thrives just as easily in abundance. Someone can have wealth, status, access—more than they once imagined—and still feel the same low-grade anxiety humming underneath everything. The mind recalibrates quickly. What was once "more than enough" becomes the new baseline, and from there, the question quietly returns: *but what if it disappears? What if this still isn't enough?*

From the outside, this can look like greed. Accumulation without end. Restlessness is disguised as ambition. But internally, it feels less like wanting more and more like bracing for loss. It's protective, almost. A belief—often unspoken—that having enough is temporary, fragile, and easily taken away. So, the person's system stays on high alert, scanning for gaps, for risks, for what's missing. Satisfaction becomes dangerous, because it invites complacency. This person's mind tells them that they'd better not become complacent. It's as if their mind is saying, *"We are in a war right now; you cannot relax."* Their system is telling them that complacency, in this mindset, is how you lose everything but it is really a hijacking to keep them from reaching satisfaction. It is a trick.

Over time, this makes them unable to register sufficiency. Moments that should land—achievements, stability, even joy—don't fully arrive. They're filtered through a lens of *"what's next"* or *"what could go wrong."* The present is never quite inhabited; it's evaluated. Measured. Compared, and almost always, it comes up short.

There's also a deeper layer to it, one that has less to do with external conditions and more to do with identity. For many people, the feeling of not having enough is tied to the feeling of not *being* enough. The two blur together, playing out something like this: *If I were smarter, I'd be safer. If I were more successful, I'd be secure. If I had more, I would finally relax.* Or I've heard more than one woman say of their own condition in life that they don't have a husband, therefore they don't have anyone to help them.

Will achieving those things just mentioned really be enough? Or will the finish line keep moving? If the underlying equation is flawed, there is no real finish line. No amount of external accumulation can stabilize an internal sense of insufficiency. *Greater is he that is in you* can work to your advantage or disadvantage. The voice in your head is greater than the one that is not, whether you audibly hear that voice or not, it is still speaking.

So, the cycle continues: striving, achieving, adjusting, and then striving again. Not out of joy or curiosity, but out of a kind of low-level fear. It could spring from a chronic dissatisfaction that's hard to name but easy to feel.

Breaking out of this isn't as simple as completing gratitude lists or perspective shifts, though those can help. It requires noticing the pattern itself—the way the mind keeps deferring arrival. The way "enough" is always conditional, always just out of reach. Then, slowly, experimenting with a different stance: allowing moments to be sufficient as they are, without immediately qualifying them.

That can feel unnatural at first. Even risky. But it's also where a different kind of wealth begins—not the kind you can accumulate, but the kind you can actually experience.

Exposure to "having" *can* change a person. When someone who has lived in lack experiences stability—consistent food, enough money, margin—their nervous system can settle. They don't have to grasp as tightly. Decisions can become less reactive. In that sense, *having* can interrupt the cycle of urgency and consumption.

It's not automatic, and it's not purely external. Two people can be given the same abundance, and respond completely differently. One stabilizes, builds, and adjusts, the other consumes quickly, almost compulsively, and ends up back in lack.

That second pattern isn't because they're barbaric, no, it's because their internal baseline hasn't changed. If someone is used to scarcity, sudden access can actually *amplify* the behavior of lack. They don't experience it as "now I'm secure," but more like, "this might not last, so use it now." Then they burn through it, and in doing so, recreate the very condition they came from.

It's not just *having* that changes a person. It's *becoming accustomed to having without fear.* That takes time, repetition, and often some kind of internal shift. Otherwise, *having* feels temporary, almost unreal—something to grab from rather than something to live within.

There are people who have never learned how to *have*. Not because they are incapable, but because having has never been stable enough to trust. So, when it comes, it is not inhabited, it is consumed. Quickly, sometimes wastefully, not out of disregard, but out of a deeper expectation that this will not last. In that expectation, they participate in its disappearance, returning again to what is familiar.

People can recreate their "normal," even when something different is briefly placed in their hands.

Whether someone has a lot or a little, if they *cannot experience enough*, they will live as if they don't have it.

THE POOR YOU HAVE

For most of human history, the fear of not having enough wasn't irrational; it was accurate. Entire civilizations have been shaped by famine, drought, failed harvests, and long winters that outlasted stored food. Across continents and centuries, scarcity wasn't a mindset; it was a condition. People lived close to the edge of survival, where "enough" was fragile and temporary, and loss was not hypothetical but inevitable. That reality leaves a kind of imprint.

Even now, in places and lives where basic survival is no longer under constant threat, the echo remains. The body and mind can carry forward an ancient expectation: that what you have can vanish, that security is short-lived, that you must prepare, accumulate, and guard against what might come.

When that inherited vigilance persists in environments of relative stability, the signal no longer matches the conditions. What was once adaptive becomes chronic. The fear remains, even when the famine is no longer at the door.

The poor you will always have with you; what makes a person identify as poor? Is it covetousness, comparison? Greed? Fear?

> For ye have the poor always with you; but me ye have not always. (Matthew 26:11)

That line points to something uncomfortable but true: "poor" is not only a condition—it can become an identity. Sadly, but truthfully, identity doesn't always track reality.

A person identifies as poor when their internal sense of *enough* is consistently below what they have or are. That gap can come from different places, and they often overlap.

Comparison is one of the strongest forces. Poverty, in this sense, is relative. A person may have stability, comfort, even excess, but placed next to someone with more, their experience shifts. What they have stops registering as sufficient because it no longer measures up. The reference point moves, and with it, the feeling of lack.

Fear plays a deeper role. Even without comparison, someone can feel poor if what they have feels fragile. If it can be lost, taken, or diminished at any moment, then it never quite counts as "enough." This is where the historical memory threads in—real scarcity leaves behind a mindset of vigilance. The identity forms not from what is, but from what could disappear.

Covetousness is more active—it's not just noticing the gap but being pulled by it. Fixating on what others have, rehearsing the difference, letting desire sharpen into restlessness can also lead to this feeling of not enough. Over time, that attention trains the mind to see absence everywhere.

Greed is often misunderstood here. It's less about wanting more for its own sake and more about trying to close an internal deficit that doesn't respond to accumulation. From the outside it looks like excess; from the inside it feels like insufficiency that hasn't been resolved.

Underneath all of it, there's something quieter: identification. When "I don't have enough" becomes "I am someone who doesn't have enough," it hardens. It stops being situational and starts being personal. At that point, even abundance can't fully dislodge it, because new evidence gets filtered through an old conclusion.

So, what makes a person identify as poor isn't one thing, it's the convergence of perception, memory, comparison, and fear. It's the story the mind tells about what is *enough*, and whether that threshold is ever truly met.

ACTING OUT THE SPIRITUAL CONDITION

From the outside, someone looks driven, restless, grasping—like they're scrambling for position, security--, more. It reads as ambition, or greed, or anxiety. That outward pattern can be the expression of something deeper and harder to name. "captivity of the soul," which is one way of describing a kind of inner constraint—a feeling of being bound, cut off, or not at rest.

This is a real observation that what we see on the surface often isn't the root of what's happening. There is a gap that we don't see between behavior and origin. Such as, their soul is in captivity (just saying) in spiritual reality, but in the natural they just feel like they need to scramble and claw their way through life.

Even if someone wouldn't use spiritual terms, the pattern still shows up in other ways:

- a constant internal pressure they can't explain

- a sense of never arriving, no matter what changes externally
- a feeling that they have to keep moving, acquiring, proving

So, the "scrambling and clawing" isn't random—it's adaptive. It's an attempt to resolve something internal using external means.

It's not as simple as, they act this way because they want more. It is more like, they act this way because something in them is not free. Something in their programming makes them act this way. That programming could be looked at as spiritual, generational, familial or longer term than that, ancestral. Whatever it is, it is embedded and probably has strongholds if it has been in the bloodline for three or more generations.

Of course, it's not your fault, but if all of Creation is waiting for the sons of God to appear and as sons of the Most High we can speak to Creation, calm storms, and pray for people's deliverance, then are there people that we might even identify and complain about who are waiting to be free? Shouldn't we be able to help them, provided they want help, instead of being victimized by them? We should be able to help ourselves as well as others. If not, our own situations and perhaps their stuckness or other spiritual conditions will keep playing out and to the chagrin and demise of what we would like to see as *civilization*.

A minister friend said she was visiting another friends house and a stranger broke in on them. She said the Holy Spirit told her to lay hands on him. She questioned if she heard correctly because the intruder had a weapon. She believed she did hear correctly, charged him and he became slain in the Spirit. Then in all authority, she told him to get out and never come back. He said, "Ma'am, I can't, I can't get up." So as a son of God we should be strong, do exploits, discern, and hear the Holy Spirit so we are not victims. Until we do--, well, what are we waiting for?

For the earnest expectation of the creature waiteth for the manifestation of the sons of God. (Romans 8:19)

If the issue is internal captivity, whether someone calls that spiritual, psychological, or existential, then no amount of external gain will resolve it. It just changes the scenery while the underlying condition stays intact. Individuals experience what they experience, but each individual contributes to the collective of mankind.

Drops in the ocean actually make up the ocean.

Not all striving is captivity. Not all ambition is compensation. Sometimes people are just responding to real pressures, real goals, real desires. As sons of God, conformed to the image of His dear Son, we make a far greater impact than staying passive or not using discernment and other gifts that the Lord has given us, in our daily walk.

What if the outward hunger of a *taker* is not the true hunger, or the core issue? What if the restlessness we see in extractors, the constant reaching in their daily lives, the inability to settle isn't about what's missing externally, but about something internally unresolved? Captivity means they are bound. Then you can clearly see that just giving them things--, giving them what they want, or even more of it won't fix that deeper core or root problem.

The GO-GETTERS

When I was much younger, I recall my mother constantly telling my older sister that she was a 'go-getter.' I thought that was great; if momma was pleased with that, then I decided that when I got older, I'd like to be that too. Recalling this now at the writing of this book is making me think of those who claw and grab after every little thing. Are those *go-getters?*

"Go getter" sounds like praise on the surface. It signals drive, initiative, hunger for life. But depending on what's underneath, it can also be a kind of sanctification of restlessness. It could be a way of approving the "clawing and grabbing "without ever asking *why* it's there.

As a child, you hear that and translate it simply: *this is good.* This is what's valued. This is what gets named, seen, and affirmed. Then, naturally, another question forms quietly underneath: *what about me?* Not even in a jealous way, just in a calibrating way. Where do I fit in that scale? When it's my turn, when I get to be that age, I'll become a go-getter too because that must be what is expected in this family.

Looking back, this sister seemed to have an urgency, to assuage her scarcity mindset. Because I am of the opinion now that she had that mindset even then. She had a need to secure something, to not miss out, to take before it's gone? No, it was expectancy; that was the road map, *right*?

From the outside, those two things can look identical. Both types of people move quickly. Both pursue. Both "get after it," but internally, they're very different engines. One is grounded, directional, even patient. The other is tense, reactive, unable to rest.

If a child learns that the second one is what gets affirmed, it can subtly shape how they understand value: not as steadiness or sufficiency, but as *constant reaching*.

This actually ties directly into "captivity." If someone *has* to grab at everything—every opportunity, every advantage, every resource—it can signal that they don't feel free to let anything pass. That's not abundance; that's pressure.

Momma never called me a go-getter and I don't know if that was being overlooked or if it was a compliment.

Wasn't Jacob a go-getter, supplanter, usurper, stealing that birthright? So, is this a good thing? Jacob *was* described as a supplanter, someone who grasped, who took hold, who secured advantage—sometimes by strategy, sometimes by timing, sometimes by outright taking what wasn't freely given. In modern language, you could absolutely hear someone call that a "go-getter"--someone who doesn't wait, someone who makes things happen.

The Biblical narrative doesn't present that cleanly as virtue. It's complicated, even uneasy. Yes, Jacob obtains the birthright and the blessing—but not without tension, fracture, and consequence. It's not a simple endorsement of grasping; it's almost an exposure of it.

When that story is placed next to my own experiences, which we will get into later in this book, this stops being abstract. It becomes embodied. I'm not just analyzing a concept; I've felt what it's like to be on the *other side* of someone else's "**getting**."

There's a difference between pursuing what is yours to build, and taking something already built, earned, or created and leaving them in the lurch. There is a difference between taking, securing, or maneuvering in a way that leaves someone else diminished.

From the outside, both can be labeled the same way. "Driven." "Resourceful." "A go-getter." But from the inside, especially from the one affected, it doesn't feel admirable. It feels invasive. It feels like a line has been crossed.

Jacob was a go-getter, wasn't he? Yes, when does "going and getting" become taking what was never meant to be taken? Why do we sometimes praise that? I'm sure mom didn't mean for her to take from others, but without that caveat, perhaps a young person would think, take at any cost. Your little sister? Your little sister is not your victim, but maybe she was an easy target.

While in college I lived with our eldest sister. She got married and moved out leaving me in the apartment. When she left, she gave me the living room and dining furniture. I lived there for about another year, then another of our sisters moved in. She dated a fellow and then moved out and they got married. This second sister took all the furniture that had been given to me when she left. She didn't take it to use because the husband she married already had a house and furniture. *Not* Momma, elder sister or anyone else in our family ever corrected her and she kept those things.

This is the go-getter sister doing all this going and getting. Will she change? Did she change?

In the Jacob story, transformation doesn't come through more grasping—it comes later, through wrestling, through being brought to a kind of breaking point, and walking differently afterward.

So, the pattern is: the praise of acquisition, the normalization of grasping, even at the often unseen cost, especially to others. Unlike Jacob, she never stole before or to my knowledge ever after. It was just me and those goodly furniture pieces that she took. She didn't even hide them under her tent like Achan did. She put them in storage.

If this were a pattern—if she were someone who regularly took, crossed lines, acted without regard—then it would be easier to categorize and dismiss: *that's just who she is*. But this stood out. It didn't fit. It *broke character*.

When something is out of character, it usually means it wasn't coming from someone's stable identity—it was coming from pressure, from something activated, something situational or internal that overrode their usual boundaries.

She's not a thief, but something in her, in that moment or season, was operating out of lack, urgency, maybe even fear. That can make people act in ways that don't align with who they normally are.

The "clawing" or grasping behavior doesn't have to be a fixed personality trait—it can be something that *comes over a person* when a certain internal state takes hold. Almost like a temporary narrowing of perspective where the usual sense of enough, or fairness, or even relationship gets overridden.

That's where "captivity" starts to resonate in a different way—not as a permanent condition, but as something that can *take hold* of someone, distort their behavior, and then pass… leaving everyone else trying to make sense of it.

It's nearly a mystery. How does someone who is not a thief… do something that feels like taking? What state were they in where that made sense to them? What were they trying to secure, protect, or resolve?

THE INHERITANCE OF LACK

Scarcity is rarely self-created. It is inherited. Not always through words. Not always through instruction, but through observation, repetition, and environment. A child does not need a formal lesson in lack, they come here with it and the goal of the parent is to bring them through and out of it. Else why would they scream and cry for every discomfort, even though their parents are feeding and changing them regularly. They have to learn. Yet, even from infancy and childhood, if they are not brought out of it, it remains. They only need to live around it long enough to absorb it.

They watch. They see everything, even things you don't think they see. They notice what is saved, what is stretched, what is questioned, and what is feared. Without even realizing it, they begin to adopt the same posture.

This is how scarcity travels.

A generation that experienced real lack passes down behaviors that were once necessary. Those behaviors settle into the home, into daily routines, into small decisions that seem harmless on the surface. Over time, the reason for the behavior fades, but the behavior remains.

The Great Depression (1929-1939) created a generation that had to be careful. They learned to conserve, to reuse, to make things last. There was wisdom in that. There was survival in that.

Survival habits, when carried forward without examination, can become limitations.

A child growing up years later does not experience the same lack. The environment has changed. There is food. There is access. There is opportunity.

But the atmosphere? The atmosphere still feels tight. So, the child begins to question what they see. Why are we holding so tightly? Not to be wasteful, but there is more available. Right?

Why are we saving in ways that do not make sense… when the system has changed? Sometimes the child cannot articulate it, but they feel it.

I remember watching decisions that did not add up to me—even as a child. One example stands out. My father, a smart man, had lived through hard times. That shaped him. One day, while driving on a country road, he decided that at the top of a hill, he could turn the car off, coast down, and "save gas."

Even as a young girl, I remember thinking: This doesn't make sense, because there is another hill coming and it will be in the opposite direction. Up. You may save a little in that moment, but you will need to spend again to go back up. The system had not changed. The need had only been delayed.

I did not have the language for it then. I did not know about inertia or momentum. But I could see something clearly: Saving in the moment is not the same as understanding the whole. That moment was small, but the pattern was not.

This is how scarcity operates, focusing on immediate gain, immediate protection, and immediate saving. But it often ignores long-term structure, overall flow, and the bigger system at work.

Like the man who built a house some years ago. He wanted a basement, but he adamantly refused to pay $30 extra for a sump pump. He ended up with a flooded basement several times a year.

When this kind of thinking, *save now, don't worry about tomorrow* is passed down, it creates a gap between reality and response.

The environment (today) may say, "There is enough." But the inherited mindset says, "Hold tight anyway because that's what I learned growing up, or that's what I learned by hard lessons in life.

This is where confusion begins for the next generation. They are not reacting to lack; they are reacting to the memory of it.

Memory, when unexamined, can shape behavior just as strongly as reality. Memory without God in it may always be brutal and survival level, scarcity level. Even if times were tough and money was tight, did you die? No, God brought you through.

Some people inherit scarcity and never question it. They somehow move past it. They 'get over it'. But getting over things may be impossible without God.

He restores my soul. (Psalm 23:5)

Worse, without still going through a certain scenario, the children can be programmed (in love) by the parents who suffered through the actual situation. The parents don't mean any harm, but that's how they live and that's what they teach their kids. That is what they model before them; and kids see everything. Their children may not have ever missed a sandwich--, like in life, so they don't understand why dad is stingy and mom is tight with the money. This is another way others inherit the trauma of their parents.

Inherited scarcity without lived lack, is inherited without experience. Scarcity is not always learned empirically. It can be taught, as much through instruction as through environment, tone, and repeated behavior.

Parents who have lived through lack often develop patterns that helped them survive, by conserving, stretching, anticipating loss, or preparing for what might go wrong.

Those patterns make sense in the context they were formed. They are protective.

Protection becomes programming. The issue is not the original experience or what happens next. When those same patterns are carried into a different environment—one where provision is stable, access is available, and basic needs are consistently met—they no longer serve the same purpose, but they remain, and children absorb them. The children may not understand the original situation, but they are surrounded by the parents' response to it.

They are learning it without living it. A child may never experience true lack. They may always have food, clothing, and access, but still develop a mindset shaped by scarcity. They are not learning the absence of provision, they are learning the **posture toward provision**. They are learning the wrong posture, an old posture, not one that fits today; it fits yesterday.

It's like the kid that is babysat by a grandparent becomes like that grandparent, skipping a generation.

They see how tightly things are held, how often loss is anticipated, and how quickly "not enough" is assumed and internalized.

Human love does not prevent transfer; nothing prevents transfer. This does not happen out of harm. It often happens out of care. A parent may think: "I don't want my child to go through what I went through." So, they teach caution. They model restraint. They reinforce awareness of loss.

While we should teach our children and not remove the old landmarks, without realizing it, they may also transfer the emotional weight of an experience the child has never had.

The result is that the child grows up with access, with provision, and with opportunity. Yet, internally they are still measuring, still anticipating lack, and still unsure that what is present is enough. None of this is because of what they experienced. Their parents were very successful in shielding their child in the natural, but they still inherited it from the Scarcity Mindset and related strongholds in the family.

This is a subtle form of trauma, and this is how scarcity can be passed down without actually experiencing the original event.

The memory does not transfer, but the mindset does. The environment changes, but the posture remains. The shift is at some point, this must be examined. Not to reject the past, but to recognize the difference between what was necessary then and what is true now

When the environment has changed, but the mindset has not, the result is unnecessary strain.

The truth is you do not have to carry what you did not experience. You do not have to live from a place shaped by conditions that are no longer present. You do not have to continue a pattern simply because it was passed to you in "love." You are seeing here that scarcity can be inherited. **You can inherit the mindset of lack without ever experiencing the reality of it.**

Know this: it can also be interrupted.

The children might notice the tension. They question the logic. They refuse to adopt what does not align with what they can see. That resistance is not rebellion. It is discernment. Awareness of this might just be the beginning of breaking the pattern. It's a pattern first, then a stronghold by the time it embeds into the generations.

HOW SCARCITY SHOWS UP IN EVERYDAY LIFE

Scarcity is not always obvious. It does not always announce itself as lack. It does not always show up in empty bank accounts or visible need. Often, it appears in small, ordinary moments such as those that should be simple. Scarcity might rear its head in moments that should be enjoyable, and in moments that reveal something deeper when examined closely. This is where the Scarcity Mindset really becomes visible, in everyday life--, no crisis needed.

Scarcity could have a person counting what should be enjoyed. Imagine ordering something as simple as ice cream. A small treat. A light moment. Nothing complicated, but instead of receiving it and enjoying it, the person begins to count. Count what? How many pecans are in the butter pecan ice cream? Was it more last time? Is this portion correct?

The moment shifts.

What should have been enjoyed becomes measured. When the count does not meet expectation, the person returns to the counter—not to purchase more, but to request an adjustment.

"The last time I got ice cream here there were seven pecans. Today, I only see five. Can I have some more?" Not satisfied. Not settled. Still looking. Ever looking--, for "enough."

The Scarcity Mindset does this. It will even interrupt enjoyment and replace it with evaluation. It will turn simple moments into calculations.

Now consider a fast-food restaurant. It is a place designed for ease, speed, and simplicity. Instead of approaching the counter when it is your turn to order, the process becomes an investigation. "How many ounces is the small? What about the medium? The large?" This customer is not asking, but calculating. Then they ask, "Which one gives the best value? Are there refills? Oh, free refills?" Twenty minutes later, line formed to the rear, "Then I'll get the small."

Questions are not the problem. But when every small decision becomes a calculation, the experience changes. What was meant to be quick becomes drawn out. What was meant to be simple becomes complicated.

Scarcity does this. It replaces ease with analysis. It adds stress where there should be none. It adds stress because maybe this person is not used to no stress.

Receiving Without Settling

Scarcity also shows up in how people receive--, even gifts. A gift is given. Not one item, but multiple. Gifts are thoughtfully chosen, and freely offered.

Instead of appreciation from the receiver of this gift, something else emerges. A problem is found. A flaw is highlighted. A request is made. The focus shifts from: "What was given" to "What is still not right" Even when there is more than enough available.

Scarcity does this. It struggles to land in gratitude. Sometimes the issue is not what was given, but how the receiver mishandled the gift. When something given and received is used beyond its intended capacity, as in overloaded, or overextended the item can be broken or become useless. When the gift breaks, the response is not, "How did I handle this?" It is, "Why didn't this hold up?" So, the receiver looks at the gift giver as if they should do more to keep the gift functioning, as if they are responsible for this gift forever.

There are warranties and people buy insurance for things, and there is usually a time limit on implied warranties. I have had someone to return a gift to me that they broke after 180 days as if I was supposed to do something about that. One might assume that they are the problem for something breaking after six months of use, so I assume that they should go get it fixed, not come back to the giver. I didn't make the item; therefore I don't guarantee the item.

Well, what I did was: No more gifts for that one.

Scarcity avoids ownership. It focuses on outcomes without examining behavior.

When Enough Never Registers

At its core, scarcity is not about what is present. It is about what is perceived. A person can have options and still feel limited. They can receive freely, and still feel deprived. They can be surrounded by provision and still search for more. More is not needed, but "*enough*" has not been internalized.

This doesn't just apply to things and stuff. A married man daily accused his wife that she didn't care anything about him if when they woke up in the mornings if she didn't go down a long checklist of his physical symptoms. How's your head? Your stomach? Your toenails? Any split ends? There appeared to be nothing wrong with this 35-year-old man, but he wanted a verbal physical check up from his non-medical doctor wife every morning. Perhaps he didn't feel as though he got enough attention growing up as the first born in his family with parents who tried to get pregnant nine years before he was born. What do you think? Do you think they ignored him? I don't.

These moments may seem small--, counting pecans, comparing portions, questioning a gift, overanalyzing a purchase, or requiring all the attention in the house every morning. Over time, they create something larger. They create tension where there should be ease. They create dissatisfaction where there should be enjoyment. They are the cause of strain where there should be flow.

Often, the person living in it cannot see it because to them, it feels normal, reasonable, maybe even necessary.

Most people don't respond this way. Most order their food, receive it and settle. They enjoy without measuring. They handle what they have whether it was a gift or their own purchase with care; it's called stewardship. They move through moments without turning them into negotiations.

Most don't try to suck out all the air in the room every morning declaring without declaring that it is all about them. The difference is in how they see, more than how they see what they have. Those who show real gratitude count blessings, not pecans. Those who are settled and balanced are not looking for what's wrong; they are looking for or appreciating what is right.

It's like those pictures that are usually two colors--, black and white, asking, *What do you see*? Well, you see what is either black or white, depending on if you are the type to see black or white. While there is a segment of the population who sees gray, is there some reason a person doesn't see black and white?

Scarcity does not begin in the hand. It begins in the part of the mind that sees. Well, the eyes see, so I'll say it starts in the part of the mind that interprets what the person sees. So, until the mind changes, the behavior will remain. It will stay just like that, even when there is more than enough.

GENEROSITY vs EXTRACTION

Generosity and scarcity do not operate the same way. They may exist in the same room. They may interact with each other, but they are not built on the same foundation.

One gives.

The other takes—even when it appears to receive.

Generosity is a spirit, a good one. A generous person gives because they can. A generous person gives Because they want to. That person is not threatened by greed, covetousness, or the fear of having less. They do not calculate every exchange to, *What's in it for me?* The non generous soul may not even be thinking of the other person or persons in the transaction, only, *What is in this for me?* While there is an appropriate time to be that way and to ask such questions, it is not 24 hours a day, every day.

Generous people show a certain prosperity in their souls. They do not give with hidden expectation. They do not feel diminished when something leaves their hand. They understand something simple: There is more where that came from, whether I currently have that more, or I'm expecting it in the future. Very generous people may even give of what they don't have and are content whether they receive more later, or not.

So, they give freely.

Generous people operate in a way that indicates that they know Source, and that Source is not themselves or some other stingy, needy, self-involved person. God is our Source, and He has more than enough.

Oh? You may ask. God is Source but we are not in the place of abundance; God put man out of Eden. Or, you may not say that because the awareness of being put out into toil and sweat. Perhaps every dearth is not in that person's mind thousands of years and as many generations later. They may believe that they are their own source. Or, their mother or father who gave them everything has gone on to glory and there is no one and therefore, no more. Or, they may believe that their mother and father won't give them anything even though they are still alive--, so they must fend for themselves.

Either way, God is not in the equation. That is where the problem starts, lies, and lives.

When a generous person receives, they settle into it. They appreciate it. They use it well. They live in a place of exchange, a place of life. Things come and go; they ebb and flow. Life and living are not stagnant. Provision is not stagnant or limited. God doesn't deal in dead things so generosity can be real, even a good thing, and not a punishment. Still, it would not have to be in the Bible that givers need to be cheerful, unless it had to be said.

Generous folks behave more like God than others. They do not search for what is missing. In life, and even in giving they move in the *shalom* of God. They enter into the Lord's rest. Generosity has *rest* in it.

Extraction is different, it has a whole other nature to it. It does not always look aggressive. It does not always announce itself, but it is present in the posture. Extraction is not satisfied with provision, no matter what is given. It is focused on maximizing outcome in their favor, because they somehow do not believe that they have enough, or ever will.

When generosity meets extraction, this is where tension begins. A generous person gives freely, even cheerfully. An extractive person receives, and then begins to adjust, question, or extend the moment.

A gift is given. Instead of, "Thank you. This is more than enough," or, "You shouldn't have." No, the response becomes, "Can this be exchanged?" "Is there more?" "Something is not quite right."

Where did you get this? With the emphasis on <u>this</u>, or worse, Where did you get this, with the emphasis on, **<u>you</u>**. The giver feels it immediately. The giver hears it immediately and if not for the Grace or instruction of God, the giver might just take that gift right back.

The giver discerns. I say this because the giver has a particular relationship with God and in their dynamic, God gives certain valuable gifts Himself, discernment being one such intangible gift. The giver has internal scales of weight and value where they realize the taker will appreciate this and it would be good to give this particular thing, but there is assurance that they are still who they always were, not diminished, perhaps even increased. There is still comfort of knowing there is more and God is their Source. There is still rest, even for the giver.

So, the giver is not necessarily angry with the one who has received, more like confused. Now the exchange has shifted. It is no longer simply giving and receiving to the extractor. It has become giving, then evaluating, then extending with the nerve to sometimes request more.

Sometimes there is no request. Sometimes the *where did you get this* means I want to go there myself and get more, more than you gave me, and possibly more than you have.

Over time, a generous person may begin to anticipate this. They have seen the pattern before… so many times before in so many people. So, the giver adjusts. They give more than necessary. They offer multiple options. They try to remove any possible reason for dissatisfaction. This is not out of obligation. They are trying to avoid the response they already expect: "If I give more, maybe this will settle it."

It does not.

It cannot because extraction is not solved by quantity. It is rooted in mindset. No matter how much is given, the posture remains: “What else is there?”

The Illusion of Fairness

Extraction often hides behind the language of fairness. “I just want what is right.” “I want to make sure I’m not being shorted.” “I want to get ***my*** value.”

These statements sound reasonable, but when they appear in every interaction, even in moments that require no defense, no struggle, no clawing, grabbing, or competition, they reveal something deeper. Not shrewd negotiations, but fear. Is it a fear of loss? Fear of missing out? Fear of not getting enough?

The Grace to Give and the Grace to Receive

Generosity is full of Grace. Generosity can absorb a lot, but it is not without limit. When generosity is repeatedly met with extraction, something begins to change.

The giver becomes more reserved, more selective, and more discerning. No, they have not become less generous; they have become more aware. They begin to understand that not everyone knows how to receive. Not everyone has the Grace to receive. Grace to give, Grace to receive must meet one another for a true, cheerful, incorruptible exchange experience.

Giving alone does not complete an exchange; the giver needs something unspoken from the receiver. There is Grace to give. The ability to offer freely, without strain, without fear of loss, without calculation is that Grace; it is from God.

The Grace to receive is the ability to accept, to settle, to recognize what has been given without resistance, adjustment, or extension. These are not the same, neither do they always exist together. When they do not meet, one person may give well. They may give freely, thoughtfully, without hesitation. But if the one receiving does not have the Grace to receive, something shifts. If the gift and the person and the thought behind the giving is not simply appreciated, then the moment is not properly completed.

This is when the exchange is interrupted. A true exchange is simple. A person without Grace can mess that all up.

Worse, a person with no intention of receiving can really jack things. Something is lost, the integrity of the moment. A complete exchange requires both sides. Grace to give. Grace to receive. When they meet, the result is ease, clarity, completion. There should be no strain, no extension, and no hidden negotiation.

It should be a clean incorruptible moment because it is holy. Giving is not the only Grace required. Receiving is also a Grace. Until both are present, in their purity, the exchange will not be whole.

It is more blessed to give than to receive (Acts 20:35)

More blessed, means both acts are blessed.

Generosity does not mean unlimited access. Christianity doesn't mean endless giving. No one is required to ignore patterns--, even the ugly ones. Generosity means giving from a place of strength, which always includes discernment. Discernment means recognizing the difference between someone who receives and settles and someone who receives and continues to pull.

At some point, the generous person must decide not just how much to give, but *where* to give. Generosity thrives in the presence of stewardship, but it strains in the presence of extraction.

More does not fix scarcity. Better does not fix scarcity. Even free does not fix scarcity. Because scarcity is not in the object, it is in the mindset. Until that changes, the pattern remains. There will continue to be receiving without settling, and having without feeling. Worse, there will continue to be getting, without ever arriving at *enough*. That is the Scarcity Mindset.

THE OPEN STATE OF GIVING

Giving is not only an action; it is a state. When a person is truly giving—not performing, not exchanging, not calculating—they are open. In that moment, the heart is not guarded. It is not withholding. It is not protecting itself from loss. It is not measuring what will return. It is extending.

What is within is allowed to move outward without resistance. That is openness.

There is also an openness of spirit.

In that willingness to release, there is a trust in the moment. When a person is willing to let something leave their hand and their life, they make themselves vulnerable. Not in the sense of feelings that will be hurt if the person doesn't like the gift, but a spiritual vulnerability.

This is not carelessness; it is confidence that what is given does not diminish the one who gives. Because of this openness, giving puts the giver in a vulnerable position, exposing them.

When a person gives from an open place, they are not only releasing an object, they are releasing intention, care, willingness, and trust. These cannot be measured in the same way as the gift itself, but they are present, and felt.

Receiving has responsibility. What is being received is not only what is visible, but it is also the openness from which it came. When that openness is met with evaluation, adjustment, or extension, the vulnerability of the moment is not honored. It may be known. It may be seen, but it is not respected.

Giving is not just transfer; it is exposure. When a person gives from an open heart and an open spirit, they are not simply parting with something in their hand. They are allowing something within them to be seen, without defense.

That is why giving requires Grace.

Receiving must be handled with care. Giving is an open moment. Open moments must be handled with care.

Generosity can feel draining in the wrong environment. Giving can feel "off" even when nothing is said. Some people instinctively pull back because their openness was not met properly. They may know it, but something different, something far more devastating could have happened.

WHEN OPENNESS IS MISHANDLED

Not every moment of giving is received well. When it is not, something more than the exchange is affected. A person gives from an open place. There is no defense, no calculation, and no guardedness, just a clean offering.

After that, the response comes. The gift transaction is evaluated, adjusted, extended, and questioned. What was open is met with something that does not match it. In that moment, there is a break.

It is not only the gift that is impacted, it is the state from which it came. The openness is interrupted. The willingness that was present begins to withdraw.

The giver may not <u>say</u> anything. They may remain calm. They may continue the interaction, but internally, something registers, "This was not handled well." That recognition creates a shift. After repeated experiences like this, the giver begins to adjust. They may give less freely, offer less often, and or become more selective as they hold back what would have been given openly, especially in this day and age where people hardly even say, *thank you* anymore.

This shift is not because they have changed in nature, but because they have learned what happens when openness is not met with care. Protection without hardness is where discernment begins to take form. The person does not have to become closed, but they become aware. They recognize that not every environment can hold an open moment.

When openness is mishandled, something is lost--, not just for the giver, but for the exchange itself. What could have been complete, clean being mishandled diminishes the entire event. Openness is not constant. Like trust, it is given. When it is not handled properly, it is not always offered again in the same way.

When a person gives from an open place, they are not only offering something in their hand, they are allowing access to a state within them. When that state is mishandled, the response is not always confrontation; sometimes, it is quiet withdrawal, or even an **unseen exchange.**

The result is that the giver remains, but the openness does not. The final distinction is that a person can still be generous— and no longer be open in the same way. That difference is not always visible, but it is real. Openness, once mishandled, mishandled repeatedly, becomes guarded. It only appears where it is recognized and received with care. The giver may remain, but the openness may not. Many times, the openness should not remain.

WHEN SCARCITY BECOMES UNSAFE

Not every person is dangerous in an obvious way. Some are unsafe in quieter ways that do not announce themselves, but reveal themselves over time. Unsafe does not always mean harmful in intent. It can mean unable to handle what is given. It can mean unable to recognize the value of what is received, or unable to settle into an exchange without extending it. In these ways, a person can disrupt what they do not understand.

A person shaped by scarcity is often in pursuit. They are reaching, evaluating. Trying to secure what feels uncertain. So, when something is given freely—they may not know how to receive it as complete.

They may look for more, question what is missing, attempt to improve or extend the moment. They are not necessarily malicious, so they are not trying to harm. Instead, they are selfishly, probably thinking they are stabilizing themselves. There are some who are more cruel and they want to take so another won't have. I am not primarily talking about that type in this book. I'm talking about those who don't mean any harm, or don't think they are causing harm.

When openness meets instability, this is where the tension lies. A giver is open. A scarcity mindset is unsettled. When these two mindsets meet, the response is not always aligned, and may be explosive. What is offered cleanly is not received that way.

This works in reverse too. Let's say a person is making a purchase at the market. The store is open for business, the customer is open and ready to trade, usually for money. Making a purchase from a store benefits both, but the seller usually makes a profit, in that sense it could be looked at as a gift, although that is tradition. But if the seller is an undercover extractor, that is a cheater, there will be a corrupt transaction. This is why God hates unjust scales. A false or corrupt movement can disrupt the integrity of the *exchange*.

A false balance *is* abomination to the LORD: but a just weight *is* his delight. (Proverbs 11:1)

The risk is not always visible. There may be no argument or confrontation. There may not be any obvious offense, but something is still affected.

Locks are for honest people.

WHO CAN BE TRUSTED WITH OPENNESS

Every person cannot be trusted with openness, nor should they be. Some are not yet able, they do not have the Grace. Not to be graphic but it is said that when you have intimate relations with someone you are basically saying, *Here is my soul*, do what you will, while hoping they won't do anything bad to you.

Over the millennia, that has turned out to be a gamble and a loss for many, many people. . While not the same as that relational act, this is an offering and making yourself vulnerable to another person.

So, who do you trust? I mean really trust? In this context, I don't mean loyalty. No, it is about capacity. The ability to receive without disruption. This person should be able to recognize what is given, settle into the moment without extending it, and handle what is offered without strain. This is what makes openness sustainable.

When the openness that was present is not sustained, the giver begins to recognize this is not a place where openness can remain. The open person may end up lamenting that they were ever open to this person in the first place. The same applies to the shopper who finds out that the shopkeeper is a cheater.

This could be a simple mismatch. It is not always about bad intention. It is often about mismatch. One person is settled, the other is not. One is giving, The other is trying to *get over*. Those two positions do not meet cleanly and honestly. Openness requires care. Not everyone has the capacity to hold it if they are still operating from lack. The cheater, the extractor is usually operating from the Scarcity Mindset.

So, discernment becomes necessary to recognize where openness is safe and when it is not. One must always govern oneself accordingly.

A person shaped by scarcity may not intend harm, but they can still be unsafe to the person who is open. They must learn to receive, settle, and recognize what has already been given. Not everyone can hold what you offer, even if they want to. Knowing that is not rejection; it is clarity.

Not all danger is loud. Some of it is simply the inability to handle what is given.

Who can be trusted with openness? Oh, what's the worst that could happen?

Malice. It could be so much more than malice; it could be extraction or even worse-- evil exchange.

What!

Yes, this is the worst thing that can happen even with the giver's good intentions. Most often the ones who perpetrate this kind of thing, *evil exchange*, either give you something or ask you to give them something. At that time, the spirit is not only distracted, but it could also be wide open--, trusting, never expecting the evil at play.

No, I'm not speaking dramatically.

What would be the impetus for someone to steal?

Greed. Lust. Covetousness. And you guessed it, Scarcity Mindset. It is just matter of boldness or lack thereof that will determine how far a person will go to get their way

So, look for this when seeking a person who can be trusted with openness. Look for a person who receives cleanly, not grudgingly or bitterly. You are looking for someone who does not look a gift horse in the mouth, search for what is missing or what is wrong with a gift. They also should not turn the moment into something else. They do not require *more* to feel settled. They understand when something is complete, and they allow it to remain that way.

They are steady, not desperate or moving urgently through life.

To understand when openness should exist and remain takes discernment. Openness is given where it can be held. It is given to those who have the capacity to receive it. Not everyone will have the capacity to receive a gift properly and to completion.

This is when you need discernment again especially if you are adopting a strategy of ‘killing them with kindness’ by giving them gifts to butter them up. The Bible does say that your gift makes room for you, but if you already see that gifts don’t change a person, and you’re the one giving the gifts, then stop it. If you haven’t yet started; don’t.

The fact that they didn’t change PROVES that the transaction didn’t work the way it should have. Either they have no Grace, or they are working the transaction some other way.

Openness is not for everywhere. It is for only where it can remain open. Once that is understood, there is no confusion, only clarity. Giving does not transform what is unwilling to receive.

CONSUMABLES vs TRUE RICHES

Extraction receives, but it still does not settle. It takes what is given, but looks for what else can be gained usually at any cost, as long as the cost is not theirs. It asks, "Can I get more?" Or, "Is there something I am missing out on?" They are constantly asking these types of questions, even when nothing is lacking

There are people who pursue God and the things of God. Scarcity Mindset people do not. Not everything people pursue is equal. Some things are consumed. Others remain. The difference between the two reveals how a person is thinking.

Scarcity hunts. A scarcity mindset does not sit still. It looks for opportunity. It looks for what can be gained, what can be held, and what can be increased.

More specifically, scarcity looks for what can be consumed. That is the hallmark and the error; almost everything it looks for is consumable.

It looks for money; money that can be spent. It looks for items that can be acquired; and most of those are for use now, or soon. The Scarcity Mindset is in survival mode because it believes it is surviving.

What is it surviving?

Life.

You'd have to ask the person with that mindset what they are trying to survive. They may not have any awareness that they are behaving differently or are trying to survive anything. They may not know what you are talking about at all.

The Scarcity Mindset is trying to access what can be used, and experiences that can be had. These things are not wrong, but they are temporary. They move. They diminish. Then they disappear.

Still, these consumables are pursued with urgency.

The hidden reason is that the pursuit is not always about desire. It is often about survival. In the mind of someone shaped by scarcity, the question is "What will keep me from lacking?" I have to stop this problem. I have to live! So, they move quickly. They gather. They hold tightly. They reach for more. Internally, they are trying to secure themselves. They are trying to save their lives, even when there is no immediate threat. They are seeking survival when there is no danger.

> The wicked flee when no man pursueth: but the righteous are bold as a lion. (Proverbs 28:1)

(I am not calling anyone wicked: that is a Bible verse.)

This is where the pattern becomes difficult to see. The environment may be stable. Provision may be present. Needs may already be met, but the internal signal has not changed. It still says, "Make sure you have enough." "Get more while you can." "Don't fall behind."

So, the person continues in survival mode— not because of what is happening around them, but because of what is happening within them.

While all of this is happening, something else is often overlooked. What are they not looking for? Things that cannot be consumed. Those things are true riches. they are such as Wisdom, Peace, clarity, alignment with God, and internal stability. These are not urgent in the same way daily needs or desires are to the person with a Scarcity Mindset. These things cannot be spent. They cannot be displayed. They do not create immediate evidence; but they remain.

The difference is that consumables must be replaced--, often, while true riches do not. Consumables create temporary relief. True riches create lasting stability. Consumables answer the moment. True riches address the condition.

The shift is rare. A person will not seek what they do not value, what they cannot see with their physical eyes (for the most part). There are some exceptions. Primarily they are looking for what is visible, measurable, and immediate, then what is lasting will seem secondary.

So, the pattern continues: More acquisition. More consumption. More effort to maintain what cannot remain.

At some point, a question has to be asked: "Is what I am pursuing capable of solving what I am experiencing?" Because if the issue is internal, then external accumulation will not resolve it. Only the setting changes.

Scarcity hunts for what can be consumed.

Wisdom seeks what cannot be taken.

A person can have more and more— and still feel as if something is missing. They are not chasing the wrong thing because they are careless. They are chasing it because, in their mind, they are trying to survive. Survival items are far different in appearance, use, and scale than things used in a normal life.

Some people hold tightly to what has the least value— and miss what matters most. Scarcity Mindset was never intended for man. It is designed to lead that man into error. The beginning of that error leads a man out of spiritual thinking into temporal thinking. Adam and Eve were led out of walking with God in the cool of the day to thinking about what to eat and later being ashamed. Then, as we have seen more than once in the Bible, their life conditions started to match their mindset. It was like a self-fulfilling prophecy. As their focused turned on what to eat, once out of the Garden, that was their focus—what to eat, how to grow it, how to get it.

Scarcity Mindset does not produce clarity. It does not establish truth. It does not lead to right judgment. It distorts. Under scarcity, a person misreads what is present, overvalues what is missing, and makes moves from pressure instead of understanding. Decisions become reactive. Perception becomes unstable. What is already given is no longer recognized or appreciated.

Scarcity does not leave a person where they are. It moves them. They fall out of alignment and into misjudgment and error. If left unchallenged, it will continue to lead a person away from what is true— and all for nothing. Even when nothing is actually missing.

Scarcity mindset was never intended for man. It is designed to lead that man into error.

THE *PERFORMANCE* OF ABUNDANCE

Not all displays of abundance are real. Some are curated. Some are intentional. Some are responses to something deeper that has not been resolved. What does this have to do with Scarcity Mentality?

Everything.

Life becomes a showcase usually to compensate for something or other. There is a difference between living well, and needing others to *see* that you are living well.

One is internal. The other is external.

In today's world, moments are often shared, recorded, and presented. There is nothing inherently wrong with that. Celebrating milestones, sharing joy, and documenting life can be meaningful. But when every moment becomes a stage, something shifts. The focus is no longer the moment itself. It becomes the presentation of the moment.

Here is the story of the *additions*. A child is playing; a baby is learning to crawl. Adorable. Nearby, placed just within view, is something expensive that usually has to do with the adult parents, and not the child. The setting includes a newly purchased item, still in its packaging, highlighted in the frame. It's not accidental; there is something new every video and that means regularly.

A simple interaction becomes layered with signals. It is quickly noticed where it came from, what it cost, and what it represents. These additions are not always spoken directly, but sometimes they are. Well, they are definitely seen.

Over time, these 'props' become consistently present. There is a message behind these moments. When this happens repeatedly, the content carries two messages at once:

1. "Look at this moment."
2. "Look at what we have."

The second message does not always need words because it is communicated through placement, emphasis, and repetition. When it becomes a pattern, it reveals something deeper.

What?

Abundance and display are integrated in thee videos, but they are not the same thing. True abundance does not need constant reinforcement. It does not require strategic placement, repeated emphasis, or visible proof in every interaction. Some of the richest people I've ever met drive knock-around cars or trucks and are often seen in the same outfit over and over. A pair of jeans or chinos and a polo and sometimes those garments are the worse for wear. Why? Because they are not fascinated with things, stuff, money, or even abundance. That doesn't mean that they never were, it's just that they aren't now. Well, at least not when I saw them.

It simply *is*. Their comfort in their relationship with sufficiency or even abundance is evident in their ease, stability, and lack of urgency to prove anything at all. They do not perform or show wealth, although they have it *like that.*

Display, on the other hand, is different. It is intentional. It is aware of the viewer. It includes signals that say, "Notice this." Sometimes the performance is not just visual. Sometimes it is verbal. In these '*kideos,*" a child is playing with an object that is obviously not a child's toy, although they are surrounded by an excess of toys. The child likes their toys, but the adult responds, speaking of the adult item, "I'll get you one." "I'll buy you that." "I'll get you something even bigger."

The moment shifts--, again. So, instead of allowing the child to simply explore and enjoy, the focus moves to acquisition. It moves to what can be given next, or added, even when nothing is missing and the child is not fretting or asking for anything at all. The child is content.

Is the parent offering what they call, love because that is what the parent would have wanted? Everything? Was that desire for everything to compensate for the feeling of having nothing, or not enough in their own past or childhood?

At its core, the performance of abundance is not about the object; it is about the need for recognition. The need for others to see it, acknowledge it, validate it. How long does this validation last? Forever, or until the next empty or Scarcity Mindset feeling?

Something is missing in the soul.

When abundance is internalized, it does not need witnesses, but when it is not, it often seeks them.

The environment creates a kind of pattern that does more than communicate to others. It shapes the environment of those within it. A child growing up in this atmosphere learns that value is visible, shiny. Possessions are signals. Moments are opportunities to show. They may not be taught this directly, but they absorb it. Over time, it becomes normal.

There are also environments where abundance is present, but not performed. Where moments are enjoyed without being framed. Where provision exists without being highlighted. Where value is understood without being displayed. These environments feel different. They feel grounded, steady, and unforced, because nothing is trying to prove itself.

The *performance* of abundance raises a simple question, is this being lived, or is this being <u>shown</u>? The answer matters. One leads to peace. The other leads to constant reinforcement. One is always adding, always signaling, and always needing the moment to say something more than it is.

The truth is that abundance that is secure does not perform. It does not need to. It is already established—with or without an audience.

THE ORIGIN OF DISPLAY

The biggest show off in the Bible. (that we know of) is in Isaiah 14, Lucifer is reported to have said,

- "I will ascend…"
- "I will exalt my throne…"
- "I will be like the Most High…"

That's not just pride, that's self-exaltation + display + positioning. This is essentially, "Look at me… above what I was given." This "show off' was Lucifer. It started, then expressed outwardly, and that led to his fall.

Show-off behavior is not about what is shown; it is about what is being established internally. Lucifer is desiring and planning his self-exaltation. Scarcity mindset embarks on external proving. Performance of abundance is to signal value. "I need to establish something about myself." The first show-off wasn't showing possessions—he was trying to elevate position.

Origin of display is Lucifer. (I am not calling any person, Lucifer.)

Human "showing" examples will follow. Hezekiah is display of self; he had a desire to be seen as more. Display starts as internal elevation before it becomes external presentation.

Babylon comes visiting. (2 Kings 20, 2 Chronicles 32). Hezekiah shows them all his treasures, all his resources, and everything in his house. No one asked for a tour like that. No one asked for a display of wealth, or capacity, or for a display of "what I have." Hezekiah's performance of abundance was the downfall of that entire nation.

The result? The prophet tells him: everything you showed…will later be taken. Display begins when what you have becomes something you need others to see. Hezekiah didn't lose what he had because he had it; he lost it because he needed it to be seen.

We see this pattern now. People feel the need to inventory what they have and present it for others to see, often, online. Then, at the same time, they install doorbell cameras, alarm systems. In some cases, they also buy weapons to protect the house, to protect the belongings, and of course, to protect the family--, who are also online. In full view.

Display does not only involve things; it can involve people, that's why people post their prettiest things, relatives and friends online.

King Xerxes I, hosts a banquet and asks his beautiful wife Vashti to come and show her pretty self for the attendees (Book of Esther). We know the story; she refuses. That was Xerxes attempting a display of possession through a person. Trophy wife: Vashti. The structure is the same as Hezekiah who was basically saying, “Look at what I have” and showing off treasures.

Xerxes did the same. “Look at what I have,” a trophy queen. It was because of the same root: “Let me show what enhances my position.” A man or king comfortable in his position wouldn’t need to ‘enhance’ it. This is Scarcity Mentality.

Solomon’s display was more showing the Glory of all God had given him, more than display performance.

Three kings have been shown, but the first human example is Cain (Genesis 4). He brings an offering that is not accepted. Instead of adjusting, he reacts and spirals into homicide. While not flashy, this introduces comparison, positioning, and resentment. These are things that often fuel “showing” behavior later.

There was another human king “display” moment by King Nebuchadnezzar who says, “Is not this great Babylon, that I have built.” That is textbook display. It is, “Look at me” language (Daniel 4).

Display follows a pattern. There is internal elevation that then leads to external presentation that then leads to exposure without discernment. Once something is exposed without understanding, it is no longer protected in the same way.

The deeper issue is that display is not about the object. It is about the *need* behind it. The need to establish, confirm, or elevate what is already present.

The truth is that display begins when what you have becomes something you need others to see. Once that shift occurs, what was meant to be held is now being presented.

Not everything that is present is meant to be shown, especially since everything that is shown might not remain. For some, seeing it is all they need to make them decide to take it. But if you put your gold in the bank instead of around your neck. Well--

Display begins internally—long before anything is ever shown.

WHEN POSITION IS QUIET

There is another side to this.

Position that is real does not need to be performed. It does not arrive announcing itself. It does not explain what is already understood. It does not elevate itself within the moment. It is already established.

A person who carries real position does not need to instruct unnecessarily. It does not need to prove what they know. It does not need to create a moment to be seen. They move within what is already theirs, because of that, there is no urgency.

There is no need to establish. They are not trying to become something in the moment. They already are. So, there is no over-explanation. There is no unnecessary correction. There is no attempt to lead where leadership is not required.

The established person is quietly confident. There is a constancy and a steadiness. This is restraint out of clarity. This person recognizes that not every moment requires them. They know who they are and do not need to try to insert themselves into everything.

Where performance is active, position is at rest.

Where performance reaches, position remains.

Where performance tries to establish, position is already established.

Real position does not need to be seen to exist. Because of that, it is not easily disrupted. It does not break under pressure. It does not collapse when tested.

What is performed must be maintained.

What is real simply holds.

In time, the difference becomes clear, not by what is said, but by what remains.

THE PENNY

This is the story of two siblings who share a utility bill. It is in the name of the sister who is grandfathered in with a good rate. When the bill comes each month, if the bill amount is an even number, she takes her time to pay it. If it is an odd number, she pays it quickly, leaving the penny remainder for the other sister to pay. In this way, even though it's a penny; she pays less. It is never just about the amount. It is about what the amount reveals.

In one setting, a person moves quickly to ensure that even a single penny is not theirs to cover. They calculate, adjust, and position themselves to avoid even the smallest excess. The goal is precision, not generosity.

In the Gospel of Matthew, there is a parable involving a penny. Workers are hired at different times throughout the day—some early, some late—and at the end, they are all paid the same: a penny. Those who worked longer begin to object. They measure, compare, and calculate what they believe is fair.

The issue is not the penny. It is the perception. They cannot receive what was agreed upon as enough because someone else received the same.

In one case, a penny is avoided. In another, a penny is rejected. But in both cases, the response is the same: “This is not right. This is not enough. This is not fair.”

A penny will reveal what abundance cannot hide. It exposes a mindset. It reveals what a person values, how they measure, and whether they can settle. Because it is never about the amount. It is about whether a person can recognize, “This is enough,” and mean it.

Some people hold tightly to what has the least value—and miss what matters most. Just as in the chapter about true riches versus consumables, the one who saves the penny today is like the Pharisees who tithe to the penny on anise, cumin, and mint. Jesus told them they are missing the weightier matters. True riches are weightier than saving a penny. Generosity of spirit, kindness, loving neighbor as thyself, preferring one another were all missed in the race to pay one penny less several times a year when the bill amount is an odd number.

What an odd behavior.

ENOUGH — THE MIND THAT SETTLES

The horseleach hath two daughters, crying, Give, give. There are three things that are never satisfied, yea, four things say not, It is enough: The grave; and the barren womb; the earth that is not filled with water; and the fire that saith not, It is enough. (Proverbs 30:15–16)

The horseleach hath two daughters, crying, Give, give... ...four things say not, It is enough." This is not just poetry. It is a pattern of appetite that cannot be satisfied.

- Give, give
- More, more
- Still not enough

All those words are the language of scarcity

There are four examples, and each one represents something that never reaches completion.

- **The grave** is always receiving

- **The barren womb** is longing without fulfillment
- **The earth not filled with water** is never fully satisfied
- **The fire** consumes and keeps consuming

They don't register *enough*. They keep reaching. They are in survival mode. This verse says some systems are wired to never say "enough."

Scarcity has a voice, and its language is, "Give, give." This passage is not describing a moment, a season, or a temporary need. It's describing a condition.

Give, Give, are the words of the voice that does not settle. It does not pause. It does not recognize completion. It does not say, *This is enough*. It says, *Give, give* because nothing has been registered as sufficient. This is not about having little, It is about never arriving at enough. No matter what is gained, no matter what is added, no matter what is present, the response remains the same.

More.

A condition, not a moment. This is not temporary; it is a pattern. It is a way of processing what is received. This speaks of a system that continues to pull, even when there is nothing missing.

The result is that a person can receive, accumulate, increase, and still not arrive. The issue is not what is coming in; it is what is not settling within.

Until the voice that says "*Give, give*" is interrupted, until that voice and that need is healed, nothing will ever be enough. This is not because provision is absent, it is because recognition is.

Enough is not a supply issue; it is a recognition issue. Scarcity is restless. It moves from one thing to the next. One calculation to another. One adjustment to the next attempt at satisfaction. It does not sit still because it does not believe it can.

Enough is not a number. It is not a specific amount of money, a certain number of items, or a perfectly optimized outcome. *Enough* is a conclusion. It is the moment the mind says, "This is sufficient," and then stops. There's no more measuring or adjusting. There is no more reaching for something additional to complete the moment. *Enough* brings stillness.

A person with a settled mind can receive something… and land in it. They do not. Instead, they turn it over repeatedly. They look for what is missing. They extend the moment unnecessarily. They receive and they stay.

This is what many people have lost: the ability to arrive at provision and also satisfaction.

Some people cannot settle. For someone shaped by scarcity, settling can feel unsafe. If they've been shaped by scarcity, scarcity is running this; they must do what scarcity demands. If they stop evaluating, it may be too alarming: what if they missed something?

If they accept what is given…what if it was not the best option? If they relax into the moment, they may start to worry --what if they end up with less--, *even a penny less?* So, they keep moving. They keep checking. They keep calculating, and they keep adjusting. Not because it is necessary, but because it feels protective.

Breaking scarcity is not about getting more. It is about seeing differently. It is about appreciation and thankfulness. It is the realization that nothing is missing. It is recognizing that nobody ripped you off and you don't need to pre-rip them off, so they won't *get* you. Once that realization becomes stable, behavior begins to change.

Perhaps the previous 'extractor' will become a trusting soul.

A settled person orders and enjoys. They receive and appreciate. They use what they have without strain. They handle problems without escalation. If something does need to be addressed, they address it, but they do not turn every moment into a negotiation. They do not search for something extra to complete what is already complete.

Enough does not mean carelessness. It does not mean ignoring value or wasting resources. It means handling what you have with awareness and responsibility, but without tension. It is the difference between managing and squeezing. It is the difference between using and extracting.

When a person reaches "enough," something lifts. Time is no longer spent overanalyzing small decisions.

Energy is no longer drained by constant evaluation. Moments are no longer interrupted by the need to optimize. There is space. There is ease. There is quiet. There is freedom from the captivity, albeit it could have all been in the mind.

Scarcity can be passed down, but so can something else. A different way of seeing. A different way of handling. A different way of living. It begins when someone decides, "I will not carry this forward." Not because the past was wrong, but because the present is different.

The Decision

At some point, this becomes a choice. Not always an easy one, but a clear one. To stop measuring what does not need to be measured. To stop questioning what does not need to be questioned. To stop reaching when nothing is missing, and to say, with certainty, *This is enough.*

The truth is, enough is not found in accumulation. It is found in recognition. Once it is recognized, scarcity loses its hold. Not because everything has changed, but because the mind has.

THE BOBBY PIN PRINCIPLE

When "Mine" Starts Small

Have you ever lived with someone where everything belonged to them? Not some things—**everything**. When we were growing up, I got told on for having her bobby pin. A bobby pin. Yes—even that belonged to my sister.

Scarcity Mentality didn't start in adulthood; it was already there. As a child, everything was "hers." Ownership expanded beyond reason, and even the smallest object became territory. It wasn't just a thought, it was reported, enforced, and escalated. That's not about the object. A bobby pin has almost no value. When someone is that precise over something so small, it points to something deeper: control over environment, heightened sensitivity to "mine versus not mine," early scarcity wiring, and identity tied to possession.

Look at the consistency. Childhood: "That's mine—even the smallest thing." Adulthood: counting pecans, auditing portions, returning to counters, extracting more. Same pattern, different scale. Nothing changed but the size of the object. Scarcity is not situational, it is patterned, and it often starts early.

She had plenty of clothes—so many that she could do laundry, leave everything in a basket for a month, and still not wear what was there. At twelve, I chose a blouse, ironed it, and wore it to school. That should have been simple, but it wasn't. It wasn't about the blouse. On the surface she had more than enough, but underneath it wasn't about use, it was about ownership. Her internal rule was simple: mine is mine, whether I use it or not.

So, when I selected it, prepared it, and actually used it, I broke an unspoken system. At twelve, I was operating from function. I'm thinking, this can be worn; it's abandoned in that laundry basket. We don't even go to the same school. I'm thinking access—it's here, it can be used; so, I used it, washed it and put it back in the laundry basket and moved on. That is abundance thinking.

But that is not how it played out. Scarcity says something else: even if I'm not using it, it's still mine; your use feels like my loss; access by others reduces what I have—even when nothing is actually lost.

The difference is simple. I saw utility. Things exist to be used. She saw possession. Things exist to be held. Scarcity does not always look like having little; sometimes it looks like having plenty and still holding tightly.

That young teen guarding a bobby pin is the same adult counting pecans—not because she is trying to be difficult, but because her relationship with "mine," "enough," and "loss" was formed early and never interrupted.

And me? I was in that world, but not *of* it.

UNUSED BUT UNTOUCHABLE: EVERYTHING IS MINE

Scarcity does not always look like having little. Sometimes it looks like having plenty… and refusing to let anything move. Closets full. Drawers full. Baskets of clothes sitting untouched for weeks. Not because there is nothing to wear. But because what is there is not being used.

Yet, let someone else reach for it. Suddenly, there is a reaction. "That's mine."

Ownership without use is not stewardship. Stewardship uses, maintains, and manages. This is possession without purpose. Items are held, not handled. Kept, not utilized. Guarded, even when they are not needed in that moment.

The tension appears when someone else does something simple: They use what is available. They take a blouse, iron it, and wear it--, not to take, but to use. That is where the response comes.

In a Scarcity Mindset, use by another person can feel like loss. Even when the item was not being used, there is more than enough available, nothing is actually being taken away. The internal signal is the same "If you are using it, I am losing it." So, the response is not based on reality. It is based on perception.

Over time, this mindset grows. It does not stay small. It expands from a bobby pin to clothing, to space, to access. Everything begins to fall under the same category: Mine. It's in that slot, not because it is actively needed, but simply because it is claimed.

At its core, this is not about objects. It is about control. Control over what belongs, who can access, what can be used, and when. If that control is challenged—even in small ways—it creates a reaction that feels larger than the situation itself.

This is what makes it deceptive. From the outside, it looks like abundance. There is plenty, but from the inside, it is still operating as if there is not. Nothing is flowing. Nothing is shared. Nothing is used freely. Nothing is allowed to move without resistance.

A different mindset sees the same situation and responds differently. If something is available and not being used, it can be used. If there is more than enough, there is no need to guard. If something is shared, nothing is lost. If I put it back, wasn't it only borrowed? If I left it in the same condition—clean, was there no harm done? Isn't the understanding simply that use does not equal loss.

Scarcity does not only show up in lack. It shows up in restriction. It shows up in holding tightly to what is not even being used. It rears its head in expanding ownership beyond necessity and then in turning access into a threat.

Everything is not yours to hold. Some things are meant to be used. Some things are meant to move. Some things are meant to be shared. When nothing is allowed to move— that is not abundance.

That is captivity. That is stagnancy. Anything without flow is dead.

WHEN TAKING IS NORMALIZED

Not all dysfunction is loud. Some of it is quiet, consistent, and reinforced over time. It does not always look like conflict; sometimes it looks like patterns that no one questions.

In college, I went to live with my eldest sister. She had a child, and I was there to help. Later, she remarried and moved out, and before leaving, she gave me the furniture. It was mine. I lived with it, used it, and it became part of my space. Then another sister moved in. When she left, she took the furniture—not by mistake, not quietly, but openly. She took what had already been given to me and used by me for a year. And when it was addressed, the response from authority (our mother) was simple, "Let her have it."

At that point, the issue was no longer the furniture; it was the system. I couldn't borrow a blouse at age twelve and put it back, but she could take furniture that was given to me and there were no repercussions. This was not just selfishness. It was a structure where ownership did not hold, boundaries were not enforced, and the person who pushed got the outcome. What was given could be taken. What was established could be overridden. The one who did not push absorbed the loss.

This is where the pattern becomes dangerous—not just that someone takes, but that the taking is validated. “Let her have it.” With that one statement, a message is reinforced: ownership is flexible, fairness is optional, and resistance is unnecessary.

This was not a small thing. This was not pecans, a handbag, or a blouse. This was my living space, my belongings, my stability. The expectation was simple: yield anyway.

In some environments, certain people are never challenged; their actions are explained away, their behavior overlooked, their position protected. Over time, a message is established: they can do no wrong. It is not stated directly, but it is understood.

In these systems, timing matters. Whoever speaks first is believed. Whoever frames the situation controls the outcome. The other voice is not examined, not weighed, sometimes not even heard.

In a healthy system, ownership is clear. What belongs to you remains yours. What is given is respected. What is taken without permission is addressed. But in a distorted system, those lines blur. Something can be given to you, used by you, established as yours, and still be taken by another—openly—with permission.

At some point, something shifts internally. The issue is no longer the item. It becomes the realization that fairness is not being applied, truth is not being weighed, and your position is not being protected.

So, a decision is made—I will step back.

When a person is repeatedly unheard, they do not always argue louder. Sometimes they withdraw. They reduce engagement, limit interaction, and stop presenting themselves for misinterpretation—not because they do not care, but because they have learned the system does not respond to truth.

In a healthy relationship, absence is felt. Distance is questioned, silence is noticed, connection is pursued. But in a distorted system, a person can step back and nothing changes. That realization brings its own kind of clarity.

This is not just about individuals. It is about a structure where some voices carry more weight, some actions face no consequence, and some people are expected to yield. Over time, that structure becomes normal.

Not every system will change. Not every dynamic will correct itself. So, the question becomes: what do you do when you see it clearly? You may not be able to fix the system, but you can refuse to participate in it. You can refuse to internalize it. You can refuse to accept what is not true, carry what is not yours, or remain in positions where your voice has no standing.

When taking is normalized and fairness is dismissed, the issue is no longer individual behavior. It is the system itself. Once you see that—you are no longer confused by it.

It is God who really knows the heart of any man. It is by the Holy Spirit that the thoughts and intents of the heart are discerned. While writing this, the thought has occurred to me that the furniture that was taken, was that payback?

For what?

IKR. Could it be her idea of payback for taking her bobby pin and using that blouse all those years ago when I was 12? Well, God knows, and if I am to know, the Lord will tell me.

We must be thankful because if we don't fully understand the Scarcity Mindset because it is not something we would think to do, or perpetrate, that means it is not in us. Amen. We don't understand it because that person is not doing something to us that we would do to them, and Amen again.

WHO GETS HEARD

In every system, someone is heard. The question is not whether a voice exists. The question is: which voice carries weight?

In some environments, whoever speaks first sets the narrative. They frame the situation, define what happened, and establish what is "right." Once that version is accepted, it becomes difficult to displace—even if it is incomplete, even if it is inaccurate—because influence is already in motion.

Not all influence is earned. Sometimes it is reinforced through money, gifts, positioning, or perceived contribution. Over time, a pattern can form: the voice that brings something is the voice that gets heard. Not because it is more accurate, but because it is more valued.

This does not always look obvious. No one says, "I will believe you because of what you give." But the outcome reveals it. Some voices are received quickly. Others are questioned or dismissed. The difference is not always truth; it is influence.

A Scarcity Mindset is easily influenced. When someone is focused on what they are receiving, what they might gain, or what they might lose, their judgment can shift—not intentionally, but gradually. What is given begins to matter more than what is true.

In the Gospel of Matthew, during the temptation in the wilderness, Jesus is offered bread, power, and kingdoms. Each offer is tied to provision or position. Jesus does not respond from lack. He does not calculate the benefit or negotiate the terms. He remains anchored. Because there is no scarcity in Him, nothing in Him is reaching, and nothing in Him can be bought.

There is another side to this. There may be a person who gives but is not heard, who contributes but is not weighted the same, who shows up but does not change the system. This can be confusing because it challenges the assumption that if I give more, I will be received differently. Systems built on imbalance do not correct themselves through increased effort. They maintain themselves.

At some point, a realization forms: this is not about what I bring. This is about how the system is structured. Once that is seen clearly, the strategy changes. Instead of asking, "How do I get them to hear me?" the question becomes, "Why am I expecting to be heard here?"

That is not defeat. It is clarity.

Not every voice will be heard in every system. Not every contribution will shift every dynamic. Not every effort will be recognized equally. That is not always something you can change. What remains is this: you can know what is true, speak when it is appropriate, and remain anchored in your own clarity without needing every system to validate it.

A person who is not anchored can be influenced. A person who is reaching can be redirected. But a person who is settled cannot be moved by what is offered, because they are not operating from lack. That is the difference—not in what is presented, but in what is needed.

There was a time my mother asked me for what I considered a large amount of money. It was my mother, so I gave. Later, I found out the money had been given to my eldest sister—the same sister who was not speaking to me at the time over a relationship that was not even what it appeared to be. That moment was not about the money. It was about what it revealed. I was the source, someone else was the beneficiary, and I was not informed.

That breaks something fundamental: trust in the exchange. It reveals misdirected loyalty, hidden channels, and unequal regard. The natural expectation is that if I am asked, it is for a real need, and if I give, it is handled with integrity. But in that system, giving did not equal influence. Position still held weight, and resources flowed accordingly.

This is the missing layer. It is not just who gives or who speaks first. It is who is favored, regardless of truth or fairness. Over time, my response showed something important. I gave, I adjusted, I tried different approaches—gifts, presence, effort—and eventually, I stopped expecting the system to behave differently. That was not bitterness. That was accurate assessment.

From the chapter, ***Who Can be Trusted With Openness, taking my own advice***:

This is when you need discernment again especially if you are adopting a strategy of 'killing them with kindness' by giving them gifts to butter them up. The Bible does say that your gift makes room for you, but if you already see that gifts don't change a person, and you're the one giving the gifts, then stop it. If you haven't yet started; don't.

The fact that they didn't change PROVES that the transaction didn't work the way it should have. Either they have no Grace, or they are working the transaction some other way.

As a kid or young adult, why did I expect a parent, mother or father to manage or take authority over a Scarcity Mindset that they couldn't even see in another sibling? Especially how could they govern it when they may have been the *source* of that mindset, so it seemed maybe---, I don't know—*normal* to them?

WHEN GIVING IS REDIRECTED

There are moments when giving reveals more than receiving ever could. For example, a request is made. It appears direct. It appears personal. The response is simple. You give because of who is asking, not because it is convenient,

Later, you discover that it was never for the one asking. It was passed on, redirected, given to someone else who either doesn't like you or doesn't respect you and who did not have the gall to ask themselves. It is redirected without your knowledge or consent.

In a misaligned system, what you give does not always determine what you receive—or how you are regarded. Sometimes resources can move through a system (family) without transparency, without fairness and without changing the system itself.

In these systems, there are often unseen pathways. Resources move discreetly, though not always cleanly. Decisions are made without full visibility. What appears to be one relationship… is actually influenced by another.

So, what I thought was a direct exchange was not. It was later revealed to be a redirected one.

What kind of system allows this?

It is the system when one of authority makes a request or a demand in proxy for another without full disclosure.

Why?

Because the one who has the need has decided they are in survival mode and the one asking has decided to save their life. But the one who it is being extracted from has no idea of any of this. More pecans. More soda. More food. More money.

Why?

To save someone's life when their life may not even be under threat.

When giving is redirected without truth, the issue is not generosity; it is misalignment.

Once that is seen clearly, you no longer measure your giving by the request— but by the structure receiving it.

WHEN A GIFT IS NOT FULLY YOURS

In some households, gifts are not always given individually; sometimes they are shared. One gift may be given to be shared between two. One item may be divided. One moment may be split. On the surface, it can appear practical, but over time, a pattern emerges. Some receive fully, while others receive partially.

That difference is felt.

When there is a message beneath a gift, it is noticed. Children may not have the language to explain it. But they understand it. A gift is not just an object. It is a signal. It answers questions they may never ask out loud:

- Am I seen?
- Am I valued?
- Am I considered individually?

When a gift must be always shared, yet the person you are made to share your gift with has their own individual gift as well as partaking in yours, the message can become unclear. This is not because sharing is wrong, but it is because of how often it happens—and to whom.

For example, one child receives something of their own. An older sibling must share their one lone gift with the child who already has their <u>own</u> gift. On top of that, the younger sibling has to also share their gift with the child who already has **their own individual gift**.

Even a child can see that is not fair.

Not every gift is equal. Not because of what it is, because of what it communicates. At some point, the object itself no longer matters. It is not about what was given, how much it cost, what it looked like, how thoughtful it was, or how difficult it was to find. It becomes about meaning.

What does this gift say?

Once that question settles in, every gift becomes part of a larger story.

The quiet conclusion is that I didn't expect much. That statement is not casual. It is learned. It is the result of repeated experience. It is the mind adjusting to a pattern it has already understood. A shared gift is not always about sharing. Sometimes it is about distinction. About who receives fully… and who does not. A child may not say it, but they see it. Every time.

These differences do not go unnoticed. They are observed, interpreted and maybe internalized and stored.

Over time, they form a quiet understanding: Everyone is not being regarded the same.

Even in a family.

Some children respond by asking. Others respond by expecting. Some respond by adjusting downward. They stop expecting much. And then less. And then they stop expecting anything at all. This is not out of bitterness, but out of recognition.

It is what it is. This is how it is.

Over time, I didn't expect much. I kept thinking, there are so many kids and maybe my parents don't have enough. My statement is not casual, it was learned. It is the result of repeated experience. It is about lowered expectations.

That's a hard lesson—having to see and learn who receives fully, and who does not. Even a child recognizes that nothing is fully theirs, that they have to share all the time. If that weren't enough, they have to share with a sibling who is selfish. It's a lot. Maybe too much. A child may not say it, but they see it. They feel it. Every time. It makes you wonder how did the child who got everything end up with a Scarcity Mindset? Is anyone ever satisfied?

As an adult, one year, my mother gave me a Christmas gift. Just that one year. The other years I received nothing.

Still, in Christ, I can say, **There is abundance; there is no lack.**

THE GIFT THAT WAS GIVEN

Unto us a child is born, a Son is given. **(Isaiah 9:6)**

In the Book of Isaiah, the language is precise. A gift was given. We didn't earn it. No, it was given. What did the people do with the Gift given to them—Jesus?

Jesus, all at once, was a shared Gift given to all of mankind and, at the same time, it was and is an individual gift. We must accept Him for ourselves. He is always with us by the Holy Spirit. He sticks closer than a brother. He is everything we need and more. He is More than Enough; He is El Shaddai.

To view the stature and the posture of the Gift given should leave us all in awe.

There is a difference between what is offered and what is received. No example makes this clearer than this: a Gift was given.

When the Gift arrived, it was not recognized by all. Some received Him. Some followed. Some understood, even if only partially. But many did not. They questioned, resisted, misunderstood, and rejected—not because nothing had been given, but because what was given was not recognized for what it was.

This was not a consumable gift. It was not expendable. It was True Riches, personified. It was not something to be used and replaced. It was not something to be displayed. It was something to be received, understood, and accepted.

The issue was not absence. The issue was recognition. The Gift stood before them, and they did not see it—not fully, not correctly.

This reveals something consistent. A person can be given something of the highest value and still not receive it if it is not recognized. This is not only a spiritual pattern; it is a human one. What is given is evaluated, misunderstood, handled incorrectly, or rejected because the one receiving does not have the capacity to recognize it.

The value of a gift is not only in what is given. It is also in the ability to receive it. Grace to give. Grace to receive; it is two sided.

Before considering the Greatest Gift, it is worth observing how people handle what is already given. Even in spiritual matters, the pattern appears. In the First Epistle to the Corinthians, the gifts of the Spirit are given—distinct, purposeful, and not self-assigned. Yet people do not always receive them cleanly. Some mishandle what they have been given. Others overlook it. Some compare. Some covet what belongs to another, as if what was given to them is not enough. The issue is not the absence of gifting. It is the inability to recognize, receive, and remain settled in what has been given.

Recall that those who are constantly reaching, grasping, and extracting are not looking for what is eternal. If they were, they would not be combing the natural for temporary things. If they were willing to submit to Christ and to the process of becoming a son of God, they would not be looking for shortcuts, even to the point of taking, extracting, or stealing.

The pattern remains. A person can be given something of the highest value and still not receive it—not because it was not offered, but because it was not recognized.

A gift can be perfect and still not be received—not because it lacked value, but because it was not recognized.

The same question remains: what do you do with what has been given?

The greatest Gift ever given was also the most misunderstood: Jesus.

If the greatest gift could be mishandled, so can every lesser one. Even with this Gift, can we not be satisfied, or will we eve be crying, *Give, give; more, more?*

There is no scarcity and no lack in the Kingdom of Heaven.

PRAYER POINTS

Prayer Points – Against Dissatisfaction

1. Father, uproot every pattern of dissatisfaction within me and establish a settled spirit that recognizes what You have already given, in the Name of Jesus.
2. Lord, silence every voice that says "more, more" when You have already provided enough, in Jesus' Name.
3. I reject every mindset of lack and receive the Grace to recognize, appreciate, and rest in what is present, in Jesus' Name.
4. Father, align my perception with truth so that I am no longer driven by internal unrest or false need, in Jesus' Name.
5. Lord, establish contentment within me that is not dependent on external conditions but anchored in You, in the Name of Jesus.

Prayer Points – Against Insufficiency & Lack

6. Father, I reject every false perception of insufficiency and receive the truth that You are my Source and my supply, in the Name of Jesus.
7. Lord, break every mindset of lack within me and establish a deep knowing that I am not without what I need, in Jesus' Name.
8. I come out of agreement with every internal voice that says, "this is not enough," and I align with Your provision, in Jesus' Name.
9. Father, restore right recognition in me so that I see clearly what has already been given, in the Name of Jesus.
10. Lord, let every pattern of perceived lack be replaced with confidence in Your provision and sufficiency, in Jesus' Name.

Prayer Points – Against Feelings of "Not Enough"

11. Father, I reject every feeling and belief that I am not enough, and I receive my identity as established and complete in You, in the Name of Jesus.
12. Lord, silence every internal voice that diminishes my value, and align my thinking with Your Truth concerning me, in the Name of Jesus.
13. I break agreement with comparison, insecurity, and self-doubt, and I stand in the sufficiency You have already placed within me, in Jesus' Name.

14. Father, heal every place where I learned to feel inadequate, and restore a settled confidence that is not dependent on others, in Jesus' Name.
15. Lord, establish me in Truth so that I no longer strive to prove myself, but rest in who I am in You, in Jesus' Name.

Prayer Points – Against Thieves

16. Father, expose and remove every thief operating in my life—spiritual, relational, or circumstantial—and restore what has been taken.
17. Lord, I close every door that has allowed loss, and I establish Divine protection over all that You have given me.
18. I come out of agreement with every pattern that permits theft—whether through ignorance, misalignment, or misplaced trust.
19. Father, guard my resources, my peace, and my assignments from every form of silent or unseen theft.
20. Lord, let restoration come where there has been loss, and establish boundaries where there has been access.

Prayer Points – Against Supplanters

21. Father, expose and remove every supplanter seeking to take what You have assigned to me.
22. Lord, I reject every unlawful transfer or exchange of position, favor, or opportunity, and I stand in what You have given me.

23. I break agreement with every system, relationship, or pattern that allows displacement or replacement.
24. Father, secure my place, my portion, and my assignment so that it cannot be taken or assumed by another.
25. Lord, let every attempt to overtake or undermine me be overturned, and establish me firmly in what is mine.

Prayer Points – Against Takers and Users

26. Father, expose every taker and user operating in my life, and remove every hidden agenda and misuse of access.
27. Lord, I close every door that allows exploitation, and I establish clear boundaries over my time, energy, and resources.
28. I break agreement with every pattern that attracts or tolerates those who take without honor or reciprocity.
29. Father, teach me discernment so I recognize who is aligned with me and who is only drawing from me.
30. Lord, restore what has been taken, and surround me with those who honor, respect, and handle me rightly.

Prayer Points – Against Family Strongholds

31. Father, expose every family stronghold operating in my life, and break its influence over my mind, choices, and patterns.
32. Lord, I renounce every inherited pattern—seen or unseen—that is not aligned with Your truth, and I come out of agreement with it.
33. I break every cycle repeated across generations—whether in thinking, behavior, relationships, or provision—and I step into a new pattern.
34. Father, uproot every structure established in my family line that opposes Your will, and establish Your order in its place.
35. Lord, let every limitation, bondage, or distortion passed down to me be broken, and let a new legacy begin with me.

Prayer Points – Repentance for Taking More Than I Should Have

36. Father, I acknowledge and repent for every instance where I have taken more than was mine—whether knowingly or unknowingly.
37. Lord, forgive me for any place where I operated in excess, entitlement, or lack of restraint, and cleanse my heart from it.
38. I come out of agreement with every mindset that justified taking beyond what was given, and I choose integrity and honor.

39. Father, restore in me a right measure and a settled spirit so that I no longer reach beyond what is mine.
40. Lord, where I have taken wrongly, lead me in making it right, and establish me in truth, balance, and righteousness going forward.

Prayer Points – Against Ingratitude

41. Father, forgive me for every place of ingratitude—seen or unseen—and cleanse my heart from every form of disregard for what You have given.
42. Lord, restore right recognition in me so that I see, value, and honor what is already present.
43. I reject every mindset that overlooks provision and fixates on what is missing, and I choose to acknowledge what is given.
44. Father, establish in me a thankful heart that is settled, aware, and responsive to Your goodness.
45. Lord, let gratitude replace every form of dissatisfaction, and align my spirit with truth so that I no longer miss what has already been provided.

Prayer Points – For Discernment to Recognize Extractors

46. Father, sharpen my discernment so I clearly recognize those who come to take rather than to align.

47. Lord, remove every blind spot, distraction, or emotional bias that would keep me from seeing people and situations accurately.
48. I receive clarity to distinguish between genuine connection and hidden extraction, without confusion or hesitation.
49. Father, train my spirit to sense misalignment early, so I am not drawn into patterns that drain or misuse what You have given me.
50. Lord, establish wise boundaries in me, and give me the Grace to act on what I discern without delay or guilt.

Prayer Points – For the Mind of Christ (Freedom from Feelings & Survival Mode)

51. Father, I receive the mind of Christ, and I come out of agreement with every thought pattern rooted in fear, emotion, and survival.
52. Lord, lift me out of reactive thinking and establish me in clarity, truth, and sound judgment.
53. I reject every feeling that drives me into urgency, lack, or instability, and I choose to be led by Your Spirit.
54. Father, quiet every internal alarm that keeps me in survival mode, and settle my mind in Your peace and sufficiency.
55. Lord, align my thoughts with Your truth so that I respond from understanding, not from pressure or emotion.

Prayer Points – To Seek the Kingdom and True Riches

56. Father, align my heart to seek Your kingdom first, above all temporary and material pursuits.
57. Lord, turn my desire away from what is consumable and establish in me a hunger for what is lasting and true.
58. I reject every distraction that pulls me toward lesser things, and I choose to pursue what has eternal value.
59. Father, open my understanding to recognize true riches, and give me the Wisdom to value what remains.
60. Lord, order my priorities so that I seek You first, trusting that all else will be added in its proper place.

Prayer Points – For More Grace and Peace

61. Father, increase Your Grace upon my life, that I may walk with ease, strength, and Divine enablement in all things.
62. Lord, establish Your peace within me, quieting every disturbance, pressure, and unrest in my mind and spirit.
63. I receive Grace to function, to decide, and to move without strain, and peace that is not shaken by circumstances.
64. Father, let Your Grace cover every area where I have struggled, and let Your Peace guard my heart and mind continually.

65. Lord, settle me deeply in Your presence so that I live from a place of rest, not striving.

Prayer Points – Coming Out of Captivity

66. Father, I come out of every form of captivity—mental, emotional, and spiritual—and I receive freedom in every area where I have been bound.
67. Lord, break every pattern, thought, or condition that has held me in place, and establish me in truth, clarity, and liberty.
68. I reject every internal prison of fear, lack, and limitation, and I step into the freedom that has already been made available to me.
69. Lord, set me free from whatever has me bound, in the Name of Jesus.
70. Lord set me free from wherever I am being held captive, in the Name of Jesus.
71. Lord, buy me back from wherever they have sold me, in the Name of Jesus.

Prayer Points – Against Preemptive Retaliation (Doing Before It's Done to Me)

72. Father, I renounce every urge to act out of fear, suspicion, or self-protection, and I choose to respond from Truth, not assumption.
73. Lord, remove every expectation of harm that drives me to move prematurely, and establish patience, restraint, and right judgment within me.

74. I break agreement with every mindset that says I must act first to protect myself, and I receive the Grace to wait, discern, and move rightly.
75. Father, align my heart so that I do not repay imagined wrongs, but walk in peace, clarity, and self-control.
76. Father, I forgive every person who has taken from me—whether openly or subtly—and I release them from every debt in my heart.
77. Lord, remove every residue of offense, bitterness, or desire for repayment, and establish Peace where there has been loss.
78. I come out of agreement with every need to hold on to what was taken, and I choose freedom over attachment.
79. Father, heal every place where I felt wronged or diminished, and restore me fully without dependence on what was lost.
80. Lord, establish me in such sufficiency that I am not defined by what was taken, but by what remains and what You have given.

In the Name of Jesus, Amen.

DECLARATIONS

I am secure, rejecting Scarcity Mindset.

I have the Mind of Christ.

I am not threatened.

I am not in danger of losing everything

I give myself permission to STOP reaching.

I give myself permission to STOP optimizing.

I give myself permission to STOP securing.

I give myself permission to START becoming settled.

I give myself permission to START becoming satisfied.

I give myself permission to START being grateful.

I command my soul to bless the LORD.

This moment is complete.

I am a blessed receiver.

I am a blessed giver and it is more blessed to give than it is to receive.

I have enough.

I have more than enough.

There is abundance; there is no lack.

I am not 5 anymore. I am not a child. I do not have to relive that situation again, in the Name of Jesus.

In Christ I am a new creation.

All things are made new.

All things are made new.

ALL THINGS are made new.

I am in the world, but not of it.

I may have been born into a scarcity culture, but I am not a part of it.

Born into that family— but not a part of it.

Born into that mindset— but not a part of it.

I am a new creation in Christ Jesus.

AMEN.

WHAT YOU CARRY FORWARD

Scarcity is not always loud. It does not always announce itself as lack. It often hides in habits, in reactions, in small decisions that seem reasonable on the surface. But over time, it reveals itself—in the inability to settle, in the need to measure, in the constant adjustment of what should have been received. This is how it continues, not because there is no provision, but because the mind has not accepted it.

You have seen the pattern. You have seen it in history. You have seen it in family. You have seen it in everyday moments that others overlook. Now, you can see it in yourself—if it is there.

This is where the responsibility shifts. It is not about fixing anyone or everyone else. It's not about becoming the Scarcity Mindset police correcting every behavior you recognize. You decide for **you:** What will I carry forward?

You may not have chosen what you were exposed to. You may not have chosen the environment that shaped early thinking. But you can choose what continues. You can choose to stop measuring what does not need to be measured, to stop extracting from what has already been given, and to stop turning simple moments into negotiations. You can choose to settle.

This does not require more money, more gifts, or more things. It requires recognition. It requires the ability to look at what is in front of you and say, "This is sufficient," and mean it.

There will always be opportunities to reach for more, to compare, to adjust, to question. That will not disappear. Your response can change. You do not have to participate when that impulse comes.

Scarcity continues when it is unexamined. It breaks when it is seen clearly and no longer accepted as normal. This is not about perfection. It is about awareness. Once God shows you something He is delivering you from it, or about to deliver you from it. Once you see it, you cannot unsee it, which means you are no longer bound to repeat it.

You can live differently. You can receive and settle. You can move through moments without needing them to prove anything. Enough is not somewhere ahead of you. It is something you recognize, and once you do—you are free.

You can discern and decide very well when to be open and when to guard your, heart, mind, soul, and spirit.

When to give and when not to give, and once you do that—you are free, indeed.

AMEN.

I seal these words decrees, declarations and prayers across every dimension and timeline, past, present, and future, to infinity, in the Name of Jesus.

I seal them with the Blood of Jesus and the Holy Spirit of Promise.

Any retaliation against this author, the reader or anyone who prays these prayers, makes these decrees and declarations at any time, let that retaliation backfire on the head of the perpetrator to infinity, and without Mercy, in the Name of Jesus.

Dear Reader

Thank you for reading. Thank you for thinking. More than anything— thank you for being willing to see.

If something in these pages stood out to you, pay attention to that. This book is not about judging others. It is about seeing clearly and choosing what you will carry forward.

Shalom,

Dr. Marlene Miles

If you enjoyed this book, here are some new releases

Christ of God (*The*) 3-book series

Christ of God, (*The*) Box Set, includes all 3books

Other books on Authority:

The Emptiers https://a.co/d/heio0dO

The Wasters https://a.co/d/5TG1iNQ

The Swallowers https://a.co/d/1jWhM6G

The Devourers: Why We Can't Have Nice Things https://a.co/d/87Tejbf

Spiritual Thieves https://a.co/d/eqPPz33

Prayerbooks by this author

There are some books that are only prayers. You just open up the book and pray.

Prayers Against Barrenness: ***For Success in Business and Life***

Fruit of the Womb: ***Prayers Against Barrenness***

Beauty Curses, ***Warfare Prayers Against***
https://a.co/d/5Xlc2OM

Courts of Marriage: Prayers for Marriage in the Courts of Heaven ***(prayerbook)*** https://a.co/d/cNAdgAq

Courtroom Warfare @ Midnight ***(prayerbook)***
https://a.co/d/5fc7Qdp

Demonic Cobwebs ***(prayerbook)*** https://a.co/d/fp9Oa2H

Every Evil Bird https://a.co/d/hF1kh1O

Gates of Thanksgiving

Spirits of Death, Hell & the Grave, Pass Over Me and My House

Throne of Grace: Courtroom Prayer

Warfare Prayer Against Poverty https://a.co/d/bZ61lYu

FAKE FRIENDS: *Prayers Against Betrayers*

HOLIDAY WARFARE Prayer Manual (humorous) Surviving Family Gatherings All Year Long (without catching a case)

SOUL TIE Prayer Manual (The) Part of a 3-part series including a workbook.

MAD at DADDY Prayer Manual – part of a 3-part series including a workbook.

Healing the Sibling & Relative Wound Prayer Manual

Healing the Father-Son Wound Prayer Manual

Breaking Curses of the Mother Prayer Manual

Other books by this author

Abundance of Jesus (The) https://a.co/d/5gHJVed

AK: The Adventures of the Agape Kid

Already Married in the Spirit: *Why You May Not Be Married in the Natural*

AMONG SOME THIEVES https://a.co/d/dkYT4ZV

Ancestral Powers

Anti-Marriage, *The Spirit of*

Backstabbers https://a.co/d/gi8iBxf

Barrenness, *Prayers Against* https://a.co/d/feUltIs

Battlefield of Marriage, *The*

BEHAVE: *Be, Then Have*

Beware of the Dog: Prayers Against Dogs in the Dream.

Bless Your Food: *Let the Dining Table be Undefiled* https://a.co/d/6oPMRDv

Blindsided: *Has the Old Man Bewitched You?* https://a.co/d/5O2fLLR

Break Free from Collective Captivity

Broken Spirits & Dry Bones

By Means of a Whorish Father

Caged Life: Get Out Alive! https://a.co/d/bwPbksX

Casting Down Imaginations

Christ of God (*The*) 3-book series

Christ of God, (*The*) Box Set, includes all three books

Churchzilla, The Wanna-Be, Supposed-to-be Bride of Christ https://a.co/d/eAf5j3x

Collateral Damage: *When What Happened Spiritually Was Your Fault*

Demonic Cobwebs (prayerbook)

Demonic Time Bombs

Demons Hate Questions

Devil Loves Trauma, *The*

Devil Weapons: Unforgiveness, Bitterness,…

The Devourers: Thieves of Darkness 2

Do Not Swear by the Moon

Don't Refuse Me, Lord (4 book series)

https://a.co/d/idP34LG

Dream Defilement

The Emptiers: *Thieves of Darkness, 1*
https://a.co/d/5I4n5mc

Entanglements: Illegal Knots Limiting Your Life

Evil Touch

Failed Assignment

Fantasy Spirit Spouse https://a.co/d/hW7oYbX

FAT Demons (The): *Breaking Demonic Curses* https://a.co/d/4kP8wV1

The Fold (5-book series)

- The Fold (Book 1)
- Name Your Seed (Book 2)
- The Poor Attitudes of Money (3)
- Do Not Orphan Your Seed (4)
- For the Sake of the Gospel (5)
- My Sowing Journal

Gang Ups: Touch Not God's Anointed

Gathered: No Longer Scattered https://a.co/d/1i5DPIX

Getting Rid of Evil Spiritual Food

https://a.co/d/i2L3WYQ

got HEALING? Verses for Life

got LOVE? Verses for Life https://a.co/d/8seXHPd

got HOPE? Verses for Life

got money? https://a.co/d/g2av41N

Has My Soul Been Sold? https://a.co/d/dyB8hhA

Here Come the Horns: *Skilled to Destroy* https://a.co/d/cZiNnkP

Hidden Sins: Hidden Iniquity

https://a.co/d/4Mth0wa

How to Dental Assist

How to Dental Assist2: Be Productive, Not Wasteful

How To Stay Prayed Up

How to STOP Being a Blind Witch or Warlock

I Take It Back

In Multiplying I Will Multiply Thee

Into Freedom:

Irresistible: Jesus' Triumphal Entry
https://a.co/d/d09IfEC

KNOW YOUR BATTLE: Stop Swinging Blindly — and Win Against Opponents, Adversaries & Enemies (Workbook) https://a.co/d/eOwFKlV

Legacy

Let Me Have A Dollar's Worth
https://a.co/d/h8F8XgE

Level the Playing Field

Living for the NOW of God
https://a.co/d/6bK5duE

Lose My Location https://a.co/d/crD6mV9

Love Breaks Your Heart

Mad At Daddy: Healing Father-Wounds that Affect Motherhood (book, workbook & prayer manual)

Made Perfect In Love

Mammon https://a.co/d/29yhMG7

Man Safari, *The*

Marriage Ed.: ***Rules of Engagement & Marriage***

Made Perfect in Love

Money Hunters: Beware of Those

Money on the Altar https://a.co/d/4EqJ2Nr

Mulberry Tree, *The* https://a.co/d/9nR9rRb

Motherboard (The) - *Soul Prosperity Series*

Name Your Seed

Occupy: *Until I Return* https://a.co/d/bZ7ztUy

One Defining Day*: A Day When Dreams Come True*

Opponent, Adversary, or Enemy?: Fight The Right Battle with the Right Weapons

https://a.co/d/byQqEE2 & companion workbook: Know Your Battle

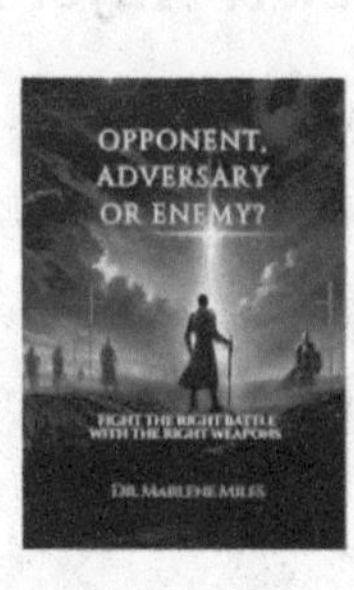

Plantation Souls

Players Gonna Play

PLEAD YOUR CASE book & Study Guide

Portals: Shut the Front Door: Prayers to Close Evil Portals.

Power Money: Nine Times the Tithe

https://a.co/d/gRt41gy

The Power to Get Wealth https://a.co/d/e4ub4Ov

Powers Above

The Robe, Part 1, The Lessons of Joseph

The Robe, Part II, The Lessons of Joseph

Scarcity Mindset (The)

Seasons of Grief

Seasons of Rest (forthcoming)

Seasons of Siege: God Is Coming

Seasons of Waiting

Seasons of War

Second Marriage, Third--, *Any Marriage*

https://a.co/d/6m6GN4N

Seducing Spirits: Idolatry & Whoredoms

https://a.co/d/4Jq4WEs

Shut the Front Door: *Prayers to Close Portals*
https://a.co/d/cH4TWJj

Siege: *God Is Coming*

Sift You Like Wheat

The Silences of God:

Six Men Short: What Has Happened to all the Men?

SLAVE

Sleep Afflictions & Really Bad Dreams
https://a.co/d/f8sDmgv

Soul Prosperity soul prosperity series 3

https://a.co/d/5p8YvCN

Soul Ties: How Soul Ties Form, and How To Break Them (book, workbook & prayer manual)

Souls In Captivity

The Spirit of Anti-Marriage

The Spirit of Poverty https://a.co/d/abV2o2e

Spiritual Thieves https://a.co/d/eqPPz33

StarStruck- Triangular Power series.

SUNBLOCK- Triangular Power series.

The Swallowers: *Thieves of Darkness*, 3

Take It Back

This Is NOT That: How to Keep Demons from Coming at You

Thrones

Time Is of the Essence

Too Many Wives: *Why You Have Lady Problems*

Tormenting Spirits https://a.co/d/dAogEJf

Toxic Souls

Triangular Power *(series),* Powers Above, SUNBLOCK, Do Not Swear by the Moon, STARSTRUCK

TRIBE: *What Covenants Are Governing You…?*

Unbreak My Heart: *Don't Let Me Die*

Uncontested Doom

Ungovered Hunger: How Unchecked Appetite Dismantles Authority

Unguarded Hours, *The*

Unseen Life, *The* (forthcoming)

Upgrade: How to Get Out of Survival Mode Toxic Souls (Book 2 of series) , Legacy (Book 3 of series)

The Wasters: *Thieves of Darkness*, Bk 2 https://a.co/d/bUvI9Jo

What Have You to Declare? What Do You Have With You from Where You've Been?

When I Was A Child, *I Prayed As a Child*

When the Devourer is Rebuked
https://a.co/d/1HVv8oq

When The Table Is Set Against You

WTH? Get Me Out of This Hell
https://a.co/d/a7WBGJh

The Wilderness Romance *(series)* This series is about conducting a Godly relationship and marriage with someone who is a Wilderness person. ***The Social Wilderness***

- ***The Sexual Wilderness***
- ***The Spiritual Wilderness***

Other Series

The Fold (a series on Godly finances)

https://a.co/d/4hz3unj

Soul Prosperity Series https://a.co/d/bz2M42q

Spirit Spouse books

https://a.co/d/9VehDSo

https://a.co/d/97sKOwm

Battlefield of Marriage, The

https://a.co/d/eUDzizO

Players Gonna Play

https://a.co/d/2hzGw3N

Sent Spirit Spouse (can someone send you a spirit spouse? This book is not yet released.)

Matters of the Heart, Made Perfect in Love https://a.co/d/70MQW3O , Love Breaks Your Heart https://a.co/d/4KvuQLZ, Unbreak My Heart https://a.co/d/84ceZ6M Broken Spirits & Dry Bones https://a.co/d/e6iedNP

Thieves of Darkness series

The Emptiers https://a.co/d/heio0dO

The Wasters https://a.co/d/5TG1iNQ

The Swallowers https://a.co/d/1jWhM6G

The Devourers: Why We Can't Have Nice Things https://a.co/d/87Tejbf

Spiritual Thieves

Red Flags: The Track Is Not Safe (book & workbook)

Triangular Powers https://a.co/d/aUCjAWC

Upgrade (series) ***How to Get Out of Survival Mode***
https://a.co/d/aTERhXO

We Get Along, Right? Compatibility for Couples – (book & workbook)

www.ingramcontent.com/pod-product-compliance
Lightning Source LLC
LaVergne TN
LVHW030922080826
845145LV00013B/3007

* 9 7 8 1 9 7 1 9 3 3 5 6 6 *